GAPOLOGY INSPIRATIONS

WEEKLY LESSONS TO HELP LEADERS
ACHIEVE THEIR GREATEST POTENTIAL

BRIAN BROCKHOFF

INSPIRED BY **MARK THIENES**

GAPOLOGY

Gapology Inspirations
REVISED 2023

ISBN-13: 978-1466494008

ISBN-10: 146649400X

BISAC: Business & Economics / Leadership

www.gapology.org

Gapology Products and Services

Visit www.gapology.org for full details on the products below, plus Gapology Institute Workshops and Coaching Services.

Books

Gapology: How Winning Leaders Close Performance Gaps

IMBAR: The Pathway of Transformation

Speed of Purpose: Achieve 2.8X Productivity and Beyond

Gapology Inspirations

Gapology Inspirations 2.0

Gapology Workbook

Also

Audible e-book: Gapology: How Winning Leaders Close Performance Gaps

Online Training Course on Udemy.com: Gapology: How Winning Leaders Close Performance Gaps

Podcast: Gapology Radio

Blog: The Gapology Angle

Social too!

Connect with us on LinkedIn, Facebook, Instagram, or Pinterest.

Table of Contents

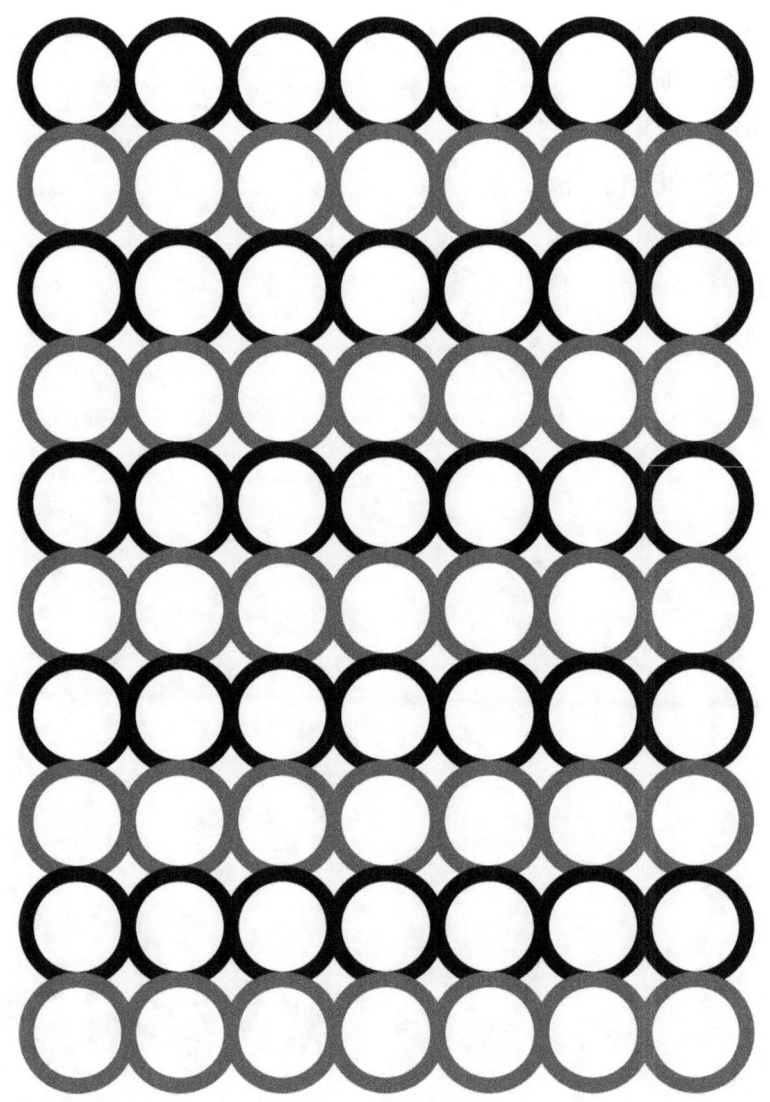

PROLOGUE

Our earlier book, *Gapology: How Winning Leaders Close Performance Gaps,* is more than just a simple book about leadership. It is a record of our journey, which has spanned over a decade and culminated in a simple yet powerful teachable method that continues to change the lives of leaders everywhere. It is a unique book because it includes a textbook-style study on the methods of Gapology, exercises to put Gapology in play immediately, and motivational stories that make Gapology real and bring these methods to life.

In this book, Gapology Inspirations, Brian Brockhoff continues the process of bringing Gapology to life by giving us fifty-two lessons inspired by Gapology. These lessons will tug at your heartstrings, make you laugh, challenge your current leadership paradigms, and strike a chord with you to continue defining the elements from the first book in a straightforward approach that you can immediately apply in your business and with the people around your life.

Brian's career has spanned more than three decades, and his work as a winning leader, trainer, executive coach, and inspirational public speaker has served him and the teams he has touched well. He has worked with many companies to improve leader and team productivity and deliver improved overall results.

He is also a devoted husband and father of three young men, and as he continues to discover each day, Gapology certainly applies to his family life as much as it does in the business world.

As you will discover, Brian's shared experiences are one of a kind, and these inspirations from Gapology will make you laugh and think and will compel you to share them immediately with your peers, team members, friends, and loved ones.

The fifty-two lessons laid out in this book are real, impactful, and instantly actionable. When speaking to your team and family, you can use them as part of your leadership rhythm or post them for others to see.

Why fifty-two? The magic of that number is that you are provided with one teachable point of view per week, which can create a simple process for building a culture of learning and continuous improvement in your teaching organization—a true leadership bonanza.

Mark Thienes

Gapology Author | CEO

INTRODUCTION

"Gaps happen."

Our groundbreaking book, "Gapology: How Winning Leaders Close Performance Gaps," lays the foundation of what leaders who consistently exceed expectations actively do to create their winning performances. We discuss the three specific Performance Gaps that they identify and close in their teams and, more importantly, in themselves.

These Performance Gaps are created when their teams don't know what to do, how to do it, why it needs to be done, when it needs to be done, or when a conscious or unconscious choice has been made not to do it.

These Performance Gaps are consistent across all industries and in all workplaces. They are not specific to any single business model. They are specific to *leadership*.

Sir Isaac Newton lays out his Third Law of Motion by stating, "To every action, there is always an equal and opposite reaction..." This foundation is as true in leadership as it is in physics. When a leader clearly leads, their team follows. When leaders train, teach, and develop, their team learns and grows. When a leader provides clear expectations and priorities, the team understands and believes in what they must do. When a leader creates a culture of commitment, the team commits. It is not a mystery. It is a scientific fact that winning leaders create winning performers.

The opposite is also true. If a leader doesn't provide quality training and doesn't intentionally teach his or her team, they won't learn and grow. If a leader skips setting clear behavioral and results expectations and clear priorities, the team won't know what is necessary to work on or work toward. If the leader ignores the importance of a culture of action, no action will be taken.

Action and reaction...cause and effect.

If a leader takes action to create the desired culture, things will happen. If they look for Performance Gaps, they will find them. If they seek ways to inspire and motivate their team, they will discover new and exciting methods. But if they don't and live a leadership lifestyle of inaction, Gaps will happen.

Gapology requires proactive leaders. They must take action. They must seek out Performance Gaps. They must probe to discover the necessary Root Solution to close the Gaps effectively and permanently. They must understand that to become a winning leader, they must practice and practice until winning leadership becomes habitual for them. If they don't...it won't. It's as simple as that. It's science.

Gapology is broken into three Performance Gaps: **The Knowledge Gap, The Importance Gap,** and **The Action Gap.** In our first book, we describe these in clear detail. For reference in this book, I've laid out the definitions below.

The Knowledge Gap

A team member or leader doesn't know what to do or how to do it. It is created by a lack of knowledge, a lack of skill, or a lack of talent.

The Importance Gap

A team member or leader doesn't know why something needs to be done or when it needs to be done. It is caused by a lack of clarity around expectations, communication, or defined priorities.

The Action Gap

A team member doesn't take action even though they know what to do, how to do it, why it needs to be done, and when it needs to be done. It is caused by a lack of accountability, commitment, and culture around taking action.

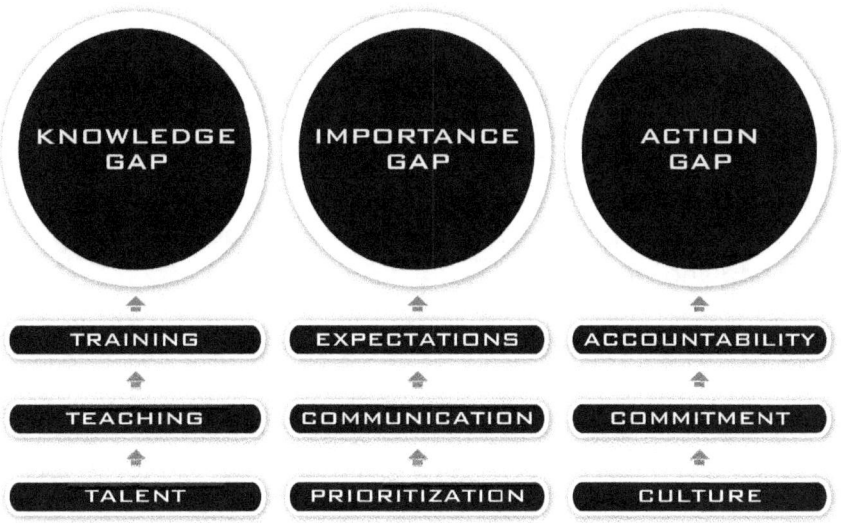

You can see in the figure above that under each type of Gap, there are specific reasons why action isn't taken. We call these areas **"Root Solutions"** because we have observed that winning leaders are proactive in their leadership, preventing many Performance Gaps from happening through an intentional process. The Root Solutions can also be applied in a reactionary method as Performance Gaps are identified.

In the book *Gapology,* we devote entire chapters to defining each of the Root Solutions and provide many exercises and tools to effectively apply the Root Solutions to prevent and close the Performance Gaps.

In this book, *Gapology Inspirations*, we're taking the model described in *Gapology* and putting it to use in a series of inspirational and motivational commentary that helps to bring Gapology to life. These articles are designed for you to use on a weekly basis. We intend you to read one each week and put its teachings around that specific topic to use in your real world. The stories have been written to be fun and interesting to read and reference but also clear enough to be able to apply the message immediately.

Read the first book as a new toolbox for your leadership. This book is a new tool for that toolbox.

In life, Gaps Happen. In the life of winning leadership, Gaps are identified and closed.

Enjoy your journey through life as a winning leader!

1 | ADVERTISING

Billions…with a "B." That is what is spent by the United States for advertising each year.

Why do companies spend it? Why do companies continue to spend this type of money in lean economies? Well, because it works.

Advertising brings customers to their doors. It gets them to spend money, which, in turn, generates profit.

This got me thinking. How do we, as individuals, advertise? What is the message or product that we are trying to sell? Are we selling the message that we are here to help our team members do their absolute best to help our customers?

As winning leaders, we need to be conscious of the message that we are advertising. Everything we do or say sends a message. We must be aware of this because our team members and customers are aware of it.

Companies advertise with a strong sense of purpose. They stop and think about the exact message they want to deliver. They think about how that message should be portrayed to describe their brand and their products or services. They spend a lot of time planning, preparing, and structuring their message BEFORE their ad is aired or printed.

Do we make the same effort in planning, preparing, and structuring our message? If not, we should reflect on how different the outcome would be if we did so. By understanding that we have a personal brand that we convey through our words and actions and understanding that if we want that brand to be one of leadership, we must intentionally determine how we will deliver that message.

Our team members should recognize that we identify and close Performance Gaps, actively communicate with them, are committed to their professional growth, and have a culture of continuous improvement. Our advertising should state that we set clear expectations, hold people accountable for their behaviors and results, and reward those who achieve the goals. Our message should be one of excellence.

Our customers should recognize that we stand for 100% customer satisfaction. They should know, by our words and our actions, that we will settle for nothing less. They should quickly recognize that each of our team members will not rest until they, as customers, are happy.

Our personal advertising should be that powerful.

Nike alone spends billions on advertising each year. Their brand is now so powerful that they don't even state their name in their ads. They often show photos and videos of athletes and then put their "swoosh" logo at the end of the commercial. Their message is clear:

they stand for high-performance sports products. They are so confident in their brand that they spend the money.

Advertising works. We just must remember that we are always advertising. We are advertising who we are, what we believe in, and who we care about.

Today, stop and think about the message you are sending and what you want it to advertise about you.

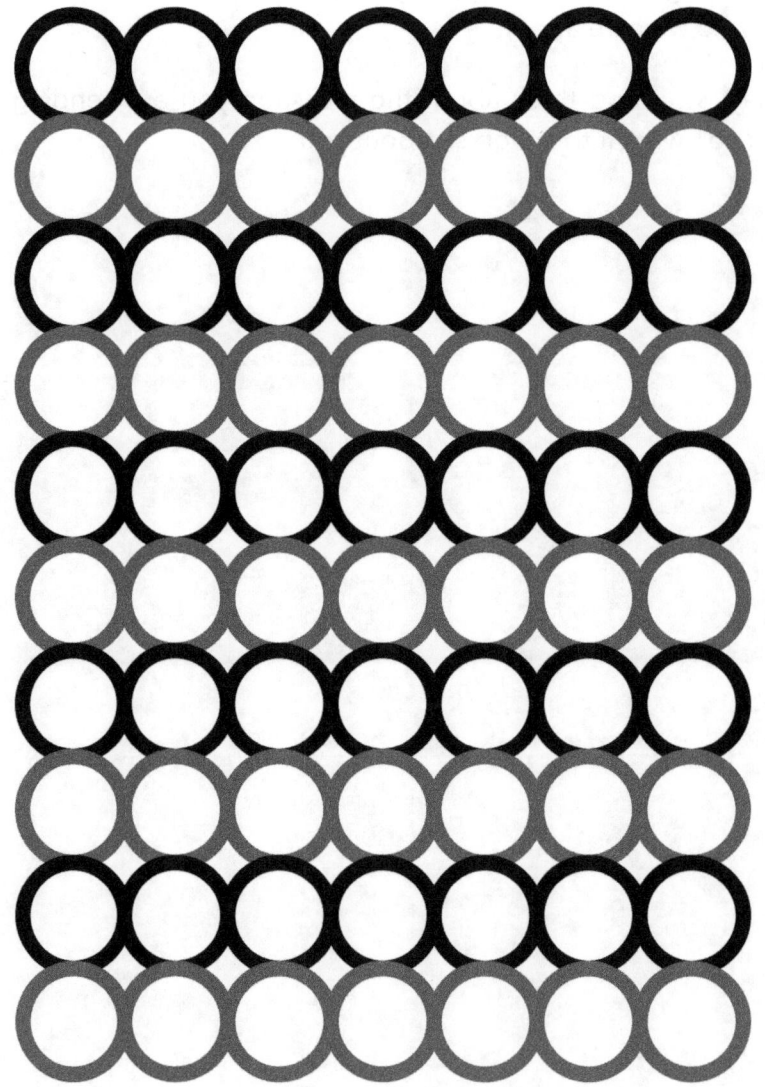

2 | AGAINST THE WIND

Today, it's snowing. The wind is blowing. The large flag outside my office window is waving in a patriotic fashion. I see the neighbors hunched over, huddled in their winter scarves and hats to fight the storm.

But just then, I see a large bird, a hawk of some sort, flying against the wind. Its head is held high. Its wings are beating furiously. And...it is moving. It's making progress against the wind. Then, just as it gets to the edge of my building, it turns its head and sails swiftly and mightily down toward its prey. Was all that struggle and effort worth it? Well, it'll be eating today, that's for sure.

This makes me think about the tremendous effort it takes to create winning leadership.

Winning leaders often must fight a wind of their own to sail as well. They may face adversity, such as cultural or ideological differences, financial or physical challenges, or multiple Performance Gaps created by other organizational leaders.

But winning leaders fight through the headwind. They flap their wings to the point of exhaustion, but they never quit. They know that, in the end, their efforts will be worth the challenge.

They start by understanding that they must begin with their own behaviors. Are they closing Knowledge Gaps with their team by ensuring that they train them to the Habit Level? Are they teaching them the meaning behind the efforts required? Are they ensuring that the talent on the team is strong enough to create the winning organization that they desire, and are they making hard choices if they discover that the answer is "no"?

Then, they ask themselves if they are doing all that is necessary to ensure that the Importance Gaps are closed. Are they setting clear results and behavioral expectations for the team? Are they using clear and concise communication and then validating and investigating whether it was received and acted upon? Are they ensuring, beyond a shadow of a doubt, that the team understands and lives the priorities and values?

And finally, they ask themselves if there are any Action Gaps. Have they transferred ownership of taking action to their team members? Are the team members making the *choice* to take action? Are they exhibiting personal accountability? Are they committed to achieving the expected results? Are they living the winning culture that is required for a winning team?

All these questions lead to work...hard work...work that will test the measure of a man or woman who wants to be a winning leader. It will challenge personal beliefs that may have been embedded for entire careers. However, open, honest self-reflection will create a bridge to stronger performance and better results, both from the leader and from the team.

Hard work, like a hawk that fights against the wind, is a challenge for us to take on. It may be difficult, especially at first, but we need to remember that in the end, winning leadership will raise us to higher heights that will let us soar!

3 | ASKING VERSUS TELLING

How do we create an environment where our team members feel a sense of ownership...one where this type of feeling of pride evolves into commitment...into motivation...into action?

People are motivated internally, and leaders must continually strive to tap into the motivational button of each team member. One powerful method we have discovered is using a technique called "Asking vs. Telling."

When providing instructions on behaviors to one of your team members, try this approach:

- Explain your objective.

- ASK your team members for their opinion on how best to achieve the objective. (Validate that the Knowledge Gap is closed.)

- ASK your team member why it would be important to achieve the objective. (Validate that the Importance Gap is closed.)

- ASK your team members for their commitment to working toward the objective. (Validate that the Action Gap is closed.)

- Explain your expectations. (Both the result expectation you want to see and the behavior expectation you want them to perform.)

Then, when you follow up with them, try this approach:

- Ask them to tell you their results.

- Ask them to tell you what the result expectations were.

- Ask what behaviors created their results.

- Ask them what the behavior expectations were.

- Ask them for ideas to improve the results.

- Ask them why they did/didn't perform to the level you had agreed to.

- Ask them for their continued commitment to perform to the expectations.

- Explain your expectations.

By following these simple steps, asking the associate versus just telling them what to do over and over will create a sense of ownership in them. *Their* behaviors are delivering *their* results.

Asking them what their results are and then asking them what behaviors delivered their results will enlighten them to the fact that they own their results. Asking them for their opinions and ideas for methods to achieve the expectations will instill a sense that they are vital, contributing members of your organization…which they are. In fact, …

- Asking pays respect to their experience level.

- Asking makes them a partner.

- Asking provides two-way communication.

- Asking builds relationships.

- Asking builds pride.

- Asking creates motivation.

There is a time and place for telling (providing instructions, explaining goals and expectations, the building is burning down, etc.), but when you want to create pride and ownership with your team, try ASKING.

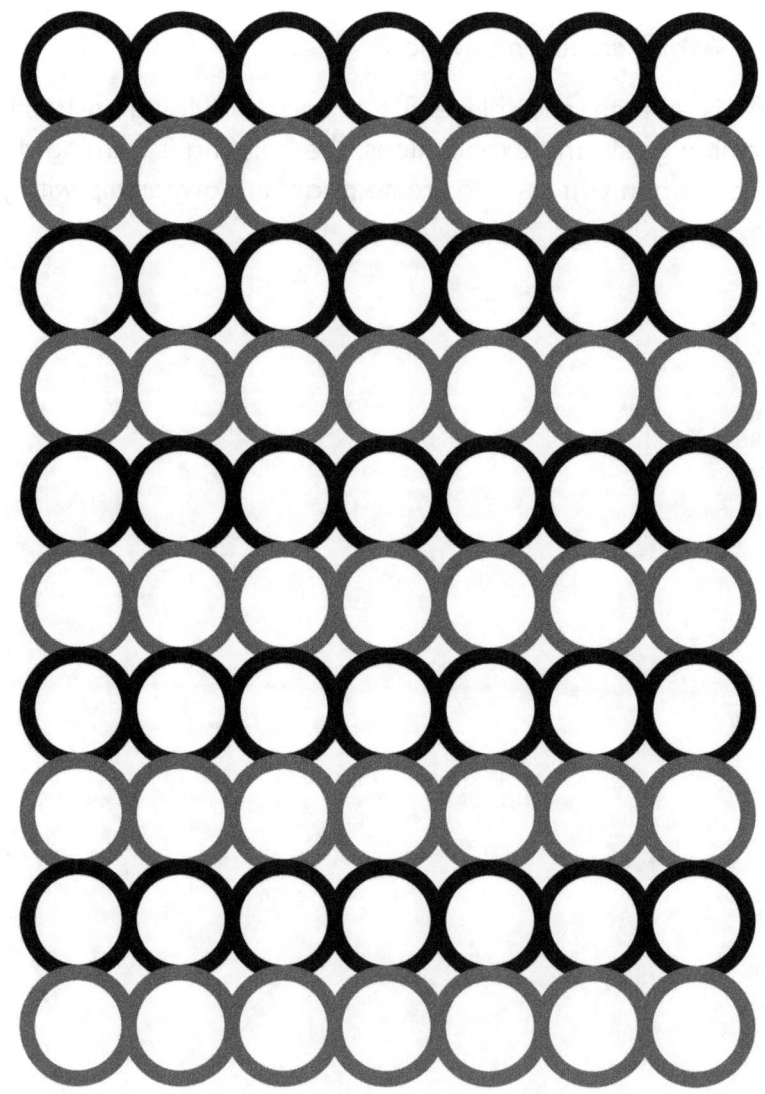

4 | BE A SPARK

The other night, during a big thunderstorm, I had a thought. How does lightning form, and why does it behave as it does?

Well, I did a little research, and basically, lightning is just a discharge of static electricity. The same thing my kids think is funny is when they rub their feet across the living room floor and then touch my cheek to shock me. This little spark is identical to what happens with lightning. Lightning is simply the same discharge of ions from one object, in this case, a cloud, to another. The interesting thing, though, is the reason for the discharge.

It is created because one object has more positive ions than the other, and the ions always flow from a positive source to a negative source or vice versa.

Ok...not to get all "scientific," but it made me think about different positive or negative sources. That is the winning leader.

Energy can flow in a team in the same way. When a leader is someone who sees the world with a positive eye, they influence others to see it the same way. They look at an obstacle as a challenge. They look at a problem as the needed solution. They consider a negative team member someone who needs to be inspired.

Positive leadership starts with an inner drive to make the world a better place, to make it someplace where people will want to work together to achieve a common goal.

When a positive leader encounters a negative team member, he or she has a unique opportunity to become a spark of positivity to them. True, meaningful positivity can spark a shift in how the team member sees and reacts to the world around them. It can completely change that person's focus from "What is wrong?" to "What can I do to make it right?"

This is a secret weapon of winning leaders. They know how to identify the negativity and create a positive spark to create commitment and develop a positive culture to achieve its objectives. They understand the importance of the spark. They believe in the power of the spark. These leaders leverage the spark to make a difference in their team members every day so that they can grow to be winning performers and experience life-altering results.

One other thing to consider is that sparks can be caused by negativity as well. Negative views, feelings, and behaviors can flow to the positive team members just as easily, perhaps even easier, than the other way around. This is a huge danger and a very large risk for any leader. Negativity must be stopped and transformed into positivity if a leader is to build positive momentum in their environment. This is why it is crucial that the leader is always looking for negativity and influencing it daily, hourly, and even minute-to-minute.

Learn more about your team by communicating with them; determine if there is negativity flowing into the team. Learn where it is coming from. Then, using your own power, build up your level of positive ions and flow that energy into the negative source to influence it and into the team to "Spark" them into a positive state.

5 | BE A STUDENT FIRST

"The best teachers are the best students."

This strong statement is important to understand and, if practiced, can create a dramatic shift in the development of our teams.

How do we become great students? First, we must be aware of its importance...it's real, true importance. Becoming a student isn't just a "nice to do" type of process; it is the first real step that is required to be a great teacher...or better yet, a winning teacher.

The winning teachers determine what it is that the students need to learn...specifically. They determine what is important. What Knowledge Gaps are holding them back? What are the things preventing them from growing? What are the things that will accelerate their learning? They determine what will dramatically impact the student's growth.

Our student's learning is what is important...and not the ego or reputation of the teacher. Teachers must put the students first and learn about them. What do they need? Why do they need it? How do they learn? What environment do they learn best in?

Understanding the answers to questions like these give the teachers the knowledge to design a learning program customized to the student's needs. It allows the teacher to give them exactly what they need, when they need it, and how they need it.

Winning leaders embrace their role as a teacher. They deliver training at a much higher level. They provide teaching and development at a much higher level. They coach at a much higher level.

Winning leaders understand that the world doesn't revolve around them; it revolves around their team members and their students. What is important is the learning and professional growth of their team.

Winning leaders become students first. They ask questions. They listen for the answers. And then they ask more questions. Discovery is paramount to them. They ask, "What are you working on?", "How are you going to do that?", "Why are you working on that?", "Why is that important?", "When do you expect it to be completed?", "Who else is involved in it?" and "What direction or support do you need from me?"

Questions like these give winning leaders an in-depth awareness of what each team member needs to succeed in their role. By asking questions, the leader can be extremely focused on the things that will dramatically impact their team.

Too often, leaders are just inspectors. They tell people what to do, and then they inspect their performance. While this is an important element of the leader's job, if the leader only remains in this role, the team members will only remain at a compliant level. They may be grudgingly compliant at worst or genuinely compliant at best. They will do what they're told, when they're told, and how they're told. While a "direct/inspect/redirect" style of leadership behavior may produce some results, it will never touch the team members' hearts to create truly committed people.

Showing that we care about our team and being curious about what they are doing, how they're doing it, and what they need shows them that we are on their side. We want them to win, succeed, and be the very best they can be. It all starts with learning about them and being a student of their human needs and their behaviors.

Start today. Ask your team SPECIFICALLY what they are doing. Ask how they are doing. Ask what you can do to help them. Don't accept the reply, "Nothing, but I'll let you know." Make them think about it. Everyone needs help at some level. They may not tell you immediately because they don't want to seem needy or weak, so be patient with them, but be persistent. The minute they share something that they need help with, do it! Following through and giving them what they need will start a momentum of support and solidify your relationship.

As a student, once you discover what they need, you can become the teacher...and deliver it.

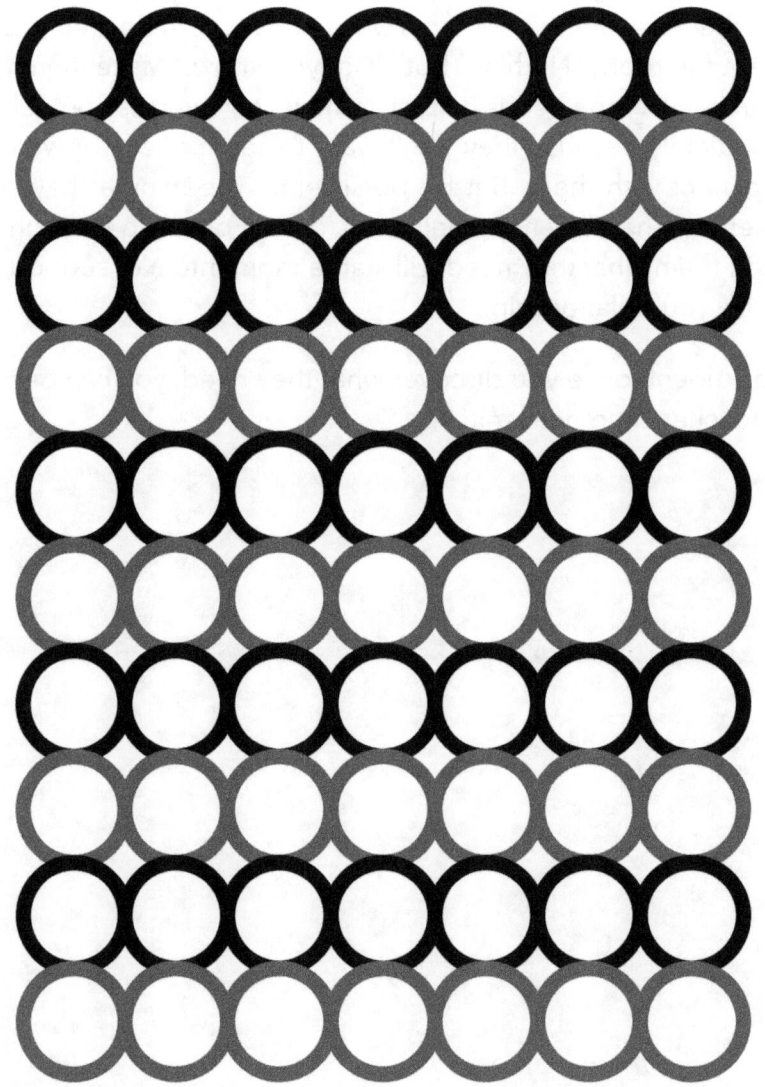

6 | BECAUSE IT'S THERE

George Mallory, the famous British Mountaineer lost in his third attempt to climb Mount Everest in the 1920s, answered, "Why do I want to climb Mount Everest? Because it's there."

Mt. Everest looms over the Himalayas like a guardian of the East. It sits above Nepal at a daunting 29,035 feet from sea level to the top of its rocky head. It has claimed countless lives and yet calls for the spirit of adventurers around the globe.

It wasn't until 1953 when Edmund Hillary and Nepali Sherpa Tenzing Norgay finally reached its summit, showing the world that even life's greatest challenges can be overcome.

In the spirit of Hillary and Norgay and their amazing journey, we look to how winning leaders attack such challenges.

As a leader of people, we all face obstacles. Mountains and valleys are a part of our everyday life. They are sometimes predictable and other times not. Our responsibility is to determine how to overcome and prevent them in the future.

In Gapology, we refer to these challenges as Performance Gaps. These Gaps can certainly appear as daunting as Mount Everest at times and often cause leaders to stumble and struggle through their careers. What winning leaders do, however, is get right back up when they fall and fight on. They don't let the rocky road steer them from their ultimate goal of winning.

How do they do it? How do they continue to move forward? They start with a strong emotional and mental commitment to succeed. They set firm expectations on the result they want to achieve and determine the exact steps that will lead to that result. Then, they follow those steps, adding new strategies and tactics along the way that help to ease past slippery slopes and leap over costly ravines.

Winning leaders struggle. They stumble. They fail. But they never fail for long. Because of their internal commitment to winning, they analyze the reasons for their failures and move forward, blazing new trails along the way. Because of this trailblazing, other leaders can look to them as an inspiration and an example of what to do and what not to do. The trails become easier to follow for those who heed their warnings along the way.

Winning leaders have demonstrated what to do to climb to the top. They have shown that Knowledge Gaps, Importance Gaps, and Action Gaps need to be actively identified and closed. Root Solutions like Training, Teaching, and Talent will set the teams up for success by creating the knowledge and skills to get the job done. They set clear expectations through solid communication and true priorities around the behaviors and results that will dramatically impact performance. They create a commitment and accountability culture where team members never dream of doing less than their absolute best. They analyze results, manage Gaps, and freely offer the rewards and consequences that celebrate and course-correct the team members who ultimately make or break the team.

They've cleared the brush and tamped down the path. They know the way. They've reached the summit. We must look to them and their example. Now, it's our turn to reach for the top.

7 | BORROWING POWER

Have you ever had one of "those" neighbors?

You know the type…the one who constantly borrows things? The one who comes over to your house every weekend and borrows a rake, a ladder, a cup of sugar, or even borrows **you** to help them move a refrigerator?

I have one of those; my neighbor borrowed my drill to hang some pictures he bought for his home…two years ago! I haven't seen it since. I guess it's much easier to borrow something than drive to the store and buy it. It's cheaper too! (Well, for them anyway…)

It does, however, make me think about something I used to do as a Retail Store Manager in my early career days. It's something called "borrowing power."

I always told my team that we had to make a change, keep to a standard, or make a sales goal because it was the "corporate policy" or my boss's idea. I would say, "Well, I'm sorry, but corporate has changed this, and we'd better follow the new process." Or "The District Manager says that we need to do things this way." or "We'd better start selling because the District Manager is coming to visit." I always borrowed their power. I never created my own.

Winning leaders are aware of this limiting language. They understand that choosing language carefully will create action and develop commitment. They know that saying things like, "I'm excited to tell you about this new program that is going to benefit all of us." or "My expectations are ..." or "I can't wait to show the boss how high our standards are!" will demonstrate the winning culture they expect.

Creating our own power by making statements that motivate our teams and show them that we are 100% committed to whatever we are trying to accomplish. We must consciously consider how we will roll out any new initiative or change direction. We must proactively look for potential Knowledge, Importance, or Action Gaps in our team. Things like word choice, tone of voice, and facial expressions all become important in how we are going to deliver the message and create a culture of winning.

Winning leaders understand that if their teams don't believe that they are completely committed and behind the message and truly believe in it, there is no way that they would get behind it either.

Even if it is controversial, winning leaders look to see its positive elements. They practice their delivery with their peers or supervisors so that their verbal and non-verbal communication comes out how they want them to.

Ultimately, we will begin to create our own power by following this process. We will feel like stronger leaders. Our team and our boss will look at us differently. Better yet, we will look at our purpose and ourselves differently. The standards and results we achieve are now because of our efforts, not our boss's.

Winning leaders create their own power; they never borrow it. Now, if I can just get that drill back...

8 | CARE

How do strong, winning leaders show that they care? When you are strong, doesn't that mean you have to be tough, cold, analytical, and feel superior?

Many leaders fall into this type of behavior. They think back to other people they've known who became leaders using methods like these and feel that the only way to be strong is to act...well...like a jerk.

The truth is...they are just acting like jerks.

Real leaders become strong by following steps that create more than just strength. These create a culture of respect, admiration, and motivation. These leaders get to know their team members individually. They learn what makes them tick, their strengths and weaknesses, what they are passionate about, and how they fit into the team. They take the time to talk to their team; they learn what they are doing, what they are struggling with, and what they are succeeding in. They identify and close Performance Gaps consistently and completely.

By learning about their team, they learn how they can help to support them and how they can help direct them. Learning about them helps to know what to train, teach, coach, and recognize.

The danger of this might be the breakdown of the authority needed to manage a team.

In part, I can see the potential danger they are discussing. By creating a more open environment, many leaders find themselves slipping into more of a friendship type of relationship with their team members. They end up going out for drinks, dancing, etc., with their team members one day and then run into big trouble when they need to hold them accountable for something the next day.

Bruce Tulgan, author of the book, *"It's Okay to be the Boss"* says that an excellent way to remember where the line is drawn is this:

"Know how many kids your team members have; just don't carry a picture of them in your wallet."[1]

The key is communication…talking. Talk to them. Schedule time to talk to them. Randomly talk to them. Just talk to them. But…talk to them about important things. Talk to them about what they like about their job. Talk to them about what they don't like. Talk about objectives, deadlines, guidelines, and expectations. Ask them how you can help them be the best they can be. Show interest in their job. Show interest in them. But…make the talking meaningful, not just conversational.

The talking doesn't have to take a long time either. It doesn't have to be a big ordeal to sit down in the office. Use the office for the private, professional conversations that need to make an impact.

Taking 2-3 minutes with each team member daily and making the communication meaningful can build relationships, identify, eliminate, and prevent Performance Gaps, and communicate clear expectations. These 2-3 minutes invested in them daily will prevent

-----

[1] Bruce Tulgan

problems and strengthen relationships like nothing else. These 2-3 minutes will show that you <u>CARE</u>.

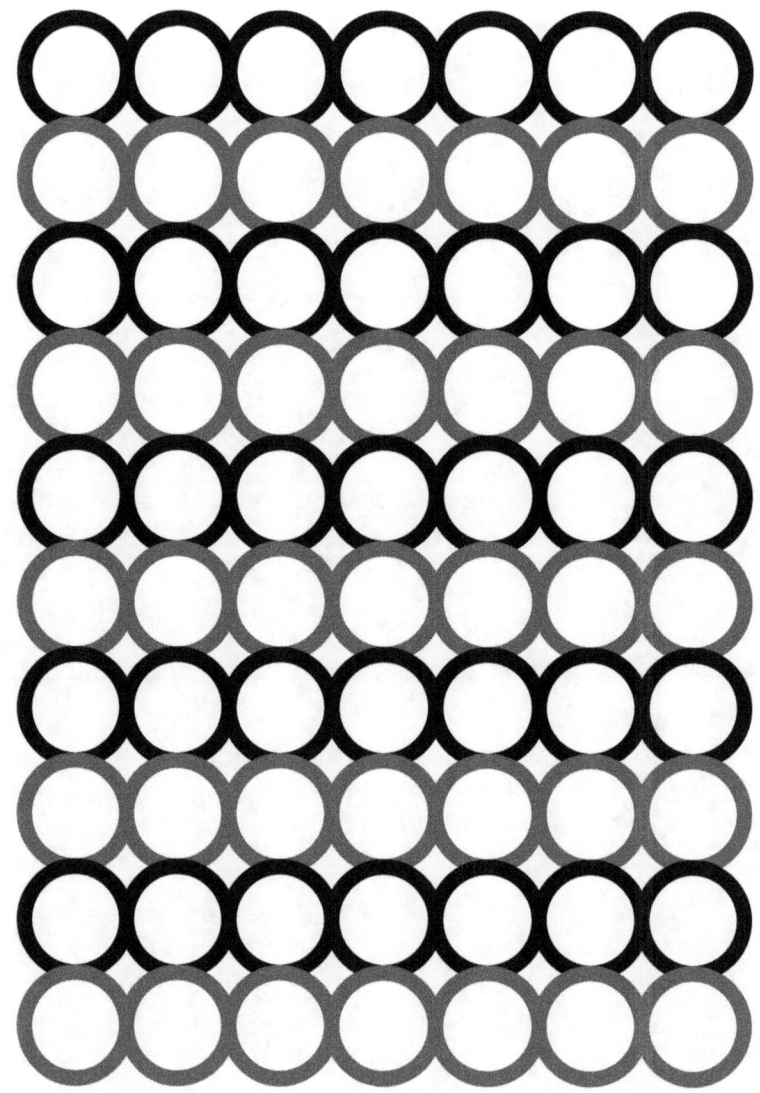

9 | CLARIFY

Some things don't seem to make sense to me. For example, my wife was buying shampoo the other day and was looking for some "clarifying" shampoo. She must have noticed the dumb look on my face, so she went on to explain that she needed a special shampoo to remove all the assorted hairsprays, volumizers, smoothing gels, curl energizing creams, straightening balms, pomades, shine sprays, oils from Morocco or wherever, from her hair. I was even more confused.

Don't you just need shampoo? I mean, isn't the purpose of shampoo to clean your hair in the first place? Why would you need something to clarify it? Am I overthinking things? Am I just a little "slow?"

Who knows? But this did get me thinking, though... As leaders, sometimes we need to clarify things as well.

When it comes to communicating expectations, we often think that our expectations are clear just because we send out instructions in an email, post a sign, or mention some directions to someone. We often muddle up significant expectations with many other things we ask people to do. We must use our own "clarifying communication" to strip away the things that may not be as important.

Importance Gaps are created when crucial elements of our business get lost in the many projects and tasks that need to get done. The whirlwind of activity gets blended with the key things that impact our business. A winning leader needs to help their team see through it all.

We must remember that the essential things cannot be casually communicated once and never reinforced. Winning leadership communication is repetitive.

We need to follow communication language like:

- "This is <u>what</u> I expect you to do and <u>how</u> I expect you to do it."

- "This is <u>why</u> and <u>when</u> I expect you to do it."

- "So... tell me what I expect you to do and how I expect it done."

- "So... tell me why it needs to be done and when it needs to be done."

- "What questions about this specific task do you have?"

- And most importantly...Use "Please," "Thank you," and encouraging, supportive words that show you care.

By using statements like these, your message will be clear. There will no longer be a shadow of doubt about what's important and whether your communication will be received in the manner necessary to get the job done. This method clarifies your expectations.

Then, as the whirlwind occurs, re-clarify and reinforce your message to let the team know that your expectations don't change.

Also, provide coaching, support, and recognition along the way to build positive momentum.

We need to think of our communication style as we think of our shampoo. Is it really doing its job? Are we effectively pouring out directions, goals, expectations, recognition, coaching, corrective action, and motivation? Is our communication like high quality, salon-brand shampoos, delivering clear support and direction to our teams daily? Or is our communication like a regular, boring generic brand shampoo, showing just enough mediocre results to get by?

If it has been the generic style, we need to really clarify our expectations and support our team! Then we will enjoy a successful team, successful results, and... well...clean hair.

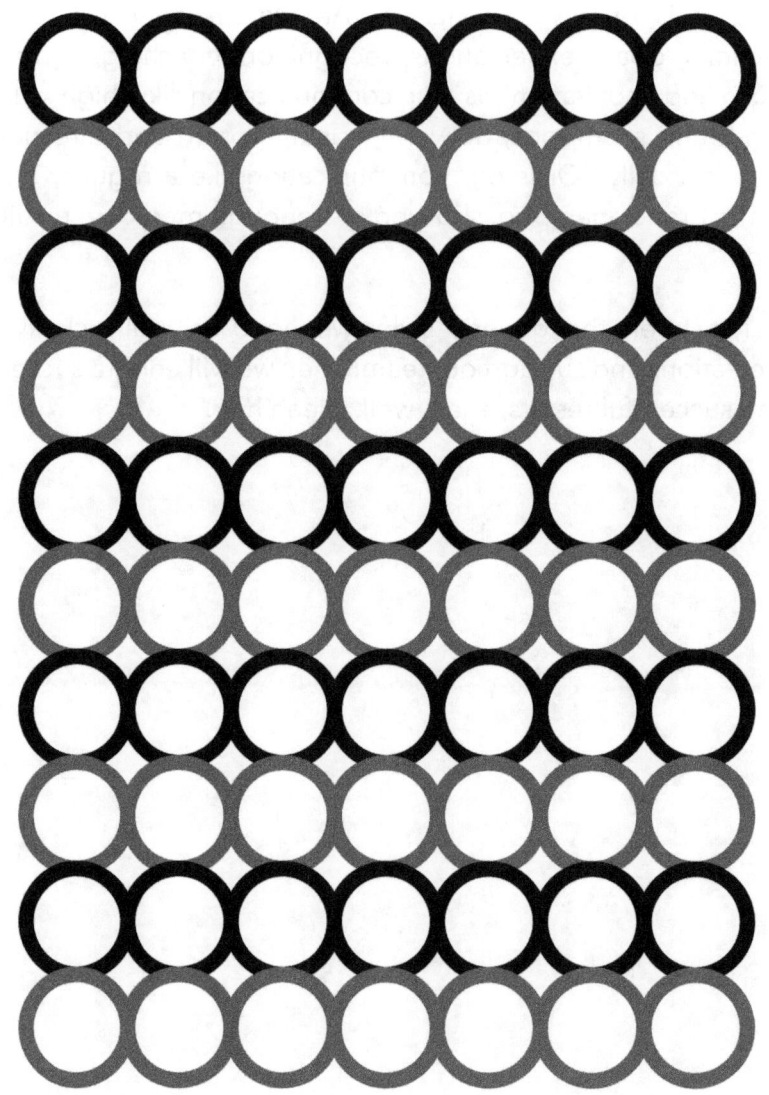

10 | CLEAN HOUSE

Moving stinks. For anyone who has ever done it, you know what I mean. Listings, showings, open houses, looking for new houses, making offers, negotiating, change of address forms, contracts, utilities, packing, moving boxes and furniture, and then unpacking. Your life becomes a whirlwind and is turned completely upside down for months.

Why do we do it? What benefits are there? For many of us, the benefits come from upsizing our homes and moving into something bigger, nicer, and fancier. For others, the benefit is downsizing, lowering monthly expenses, and having less to care for and clean. Whatever the reason, we do it.

One big benefit of moving is the opportunity to clean house. I'm not talking about dusting and vacuuming; I'm referring to deep cleaning. Going through the storage bins in the basement and garage and tossing out the old "keepsakes" that really aren't worth keeping. Old toys, old notebooks, and old clothes sit around and gather dust in the closets and crevices of our storage areas and the backs of our minds.

I love to do this, strange as it may sound, because it is the chance to start fresh. Throwing away or donating old items gives me a sense of relief and freedom. I love the "clean house" feeling.

We can apply this "clean house" feeling to our leadership roles. What can we do physically in our businesses? What cleaning can we do?

Winning leaders first look at their own behaviors. What Knowledge Gaps are they creating? What Importance Gaps are they creating? What Action Gaps are they allowing to continue? What are they doing that isn't driving results? Are they training and developing their team strongly enough so that they are creating new habits? Does the team know what to do and how to do it? Are they setting clear results and behavioral expectations? Does the team understand specifically what the priorities are? Do they know why they need to do things and when they are to be done? Do they measure results, determining what drives both the wins and the losses? Do they leverage their winning behaviors and course-correct their losing behaviors? Are they providing feedback through coaching to the team? Are they then counseling poor performance and celebrating great performance?

Winning leaders then look at the talent on their team. Who is just gathering dust? These are the people who drag down others around them and drag down the overall organization. Winning leaders understand that these people aren't contributing to their success, and when they've done the appropriate amount of coaching, counseling, and documentation, they need to replace them. They know they'll feel much better and perform better with a clean house.

How about us? Are we leading our teams to action?

If the answer is no, we must clean our house.

For us to move our teams forward, we cannot get caught up in the messes we've created in the past. Taking deliberate steps to correct them will free us from them. It will allow us to move forward instead of staying stuck in the past. It will allow us to move from negative momentum to positive momentum, and we'll begin to see and feel the wins take place.

Does moving stink? Yes...but then again, no. Short-term pain brings long-term gain. The same can be said for our leadership. Investing time today into cleaning our own houses will bring us longer-term results, and we will feel better, too!

Start cleaning today!

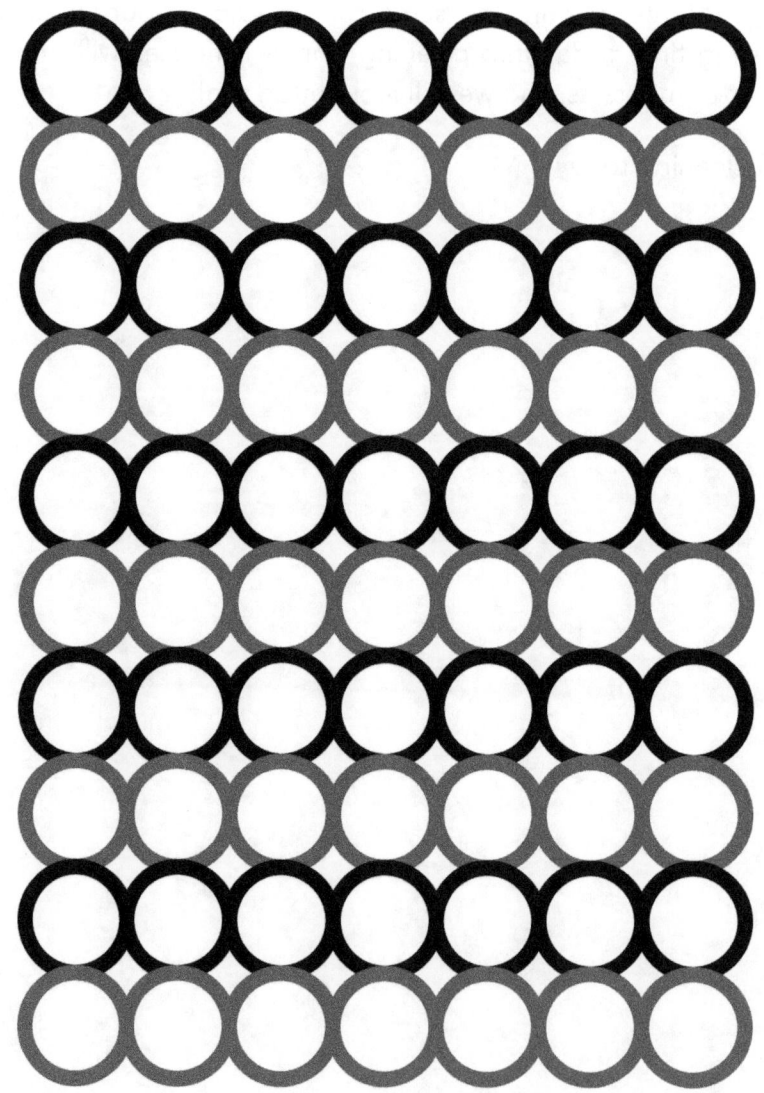

11 | COACH

When you picture a coach, who do you see? Do you see a gruff, whistleblowing, yelling, and screaming man or woman who tortured you as a young child? Or do you see a mentor, a motivator, and an inspiration?

Growing up, many of us participated in team or individual athletics. Baseball, Softball, Soccer, Tennis, Track, and Field...all impacted us because of the friendly competition, the muscle-building exercise, and our coaches.

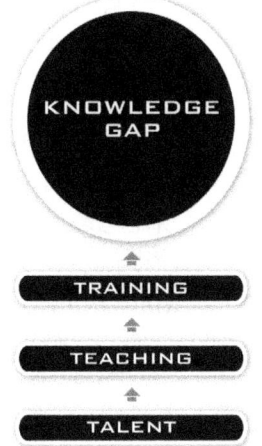

As an athlete, your coach has one role. That role is to improve the performance of the individual and/or team to achieve the desired result. That desired result is to win. As a business leader, your role is the same.

In Gapology, the Root Solutions under the Knowledge Gap are Training, Teaching, and Talent. Coaching taps into all three. Many people consider coaching to be the ultimate teaching method as it is hands-on, in the moment, and outcome-driven. Coaching is a very powerful tool for closing Knowledge Gaps.

As a leader, our coaching role is the single most important skill to excel in. If we are good at coaching, we can improve our team and move them to take action in every one of our measurable results. Our organization's current focus doesn't matter; we can win if we can effectively coach to improve performance. If we could only perform one single behavior in our whole day, and that behavior HAD to produce DRAMATIC results, it would need to be coaching.

So, what makes coaching effective? The leader must follow clear, specific steps with strength and conviction. They must be skilled in it. They must be able to demonstrate it. They must win at it.

- A winning coaching session begins with **Preparation**. The coach needs to know their team. Where are they on the Habit Ladder? Where are they on the Commitment Ladder? What Performance Gaps need to be closed? What are their strengths to celebrate and their weaknesses to develop? They need to know their commitment, confidence, and competence levels and what drives them to perform. They need to observe and document specific behaviors and results. They must know the facts.

- Next, the winning coach needs to start with a strong **Opening** that builds rapport and establishes the purpose of the session. The coach must gain the team members' buy-in at this point by communicating the importance of the team member and their role on the larger team.

- **Perceptions** (Get, Give, Agree) are given by the team member, and the coach will then provide the documented details of past performance. These are the facts. These are verifiable behaviors and results and the perceived impact on the team and the overall results. It's important to start with the team member's perceptions first. Ask them what they think. Ask them what opportunities for improvement they have and what strength areas exist. By doing this, the team members will reflect internally on their behaviors and identify potential solutions. Then, the coach needs to provide their own perceptions and observations regarding the behaviors mentioned by the team member and those not mentioned. The two then need to agree on the demonstrated behaviors, the expected behaviors, and the developmental area. This needs to be done with EDGE (Energy, Decisiveness, Greatness, and Expectations) for the coach to establish themselves as the leader.

- **Obstacles** that prevent the team member from performing the expected behaviors must be identified and removed. Again, asking the team members is the best way to discover these obstacles, and asking for their ideas to remove them is the best way to build their feeling of ownership. By asking versus telling, you validate their willingness to improve and grow and, therefore, build commitment. Once these ideas are identified, the coach must help to remove the obstacles by asking for agreement and commitment to the new behaviors.

- The **Closing** is where the action begins. In this step, the coach will summarize the agreements that were made and set specific action steps and time frames. Communicating that follow-up will occur to continue helping the team members improve. This communication helps solidify and strengthen the relationship to build long-term commitments.

- The final step is the **Follow-Up**. Follow-up establishes accountability and credibility in the overall coaching process and is done to ensure that commitment to real behavioral changes is the result. If follow-up fails to happen, the team will quickly learn that coaching has no merit in the real world and, therefore, change is optional.

Coaching is motivational. Coaching is developmental. Coaching must be a strategic part of your Leadership Rhythm, being performed consistently and constantly. It can be done in a formal environment or "in-the-moment." Coaching shows responsibility and managerial courage. It provides a competitive edge. Coaching pushes for real change and real results. Coaching requires winning leader competencies in all these areas, and when performed with EDGE, it will deliver our expectations.

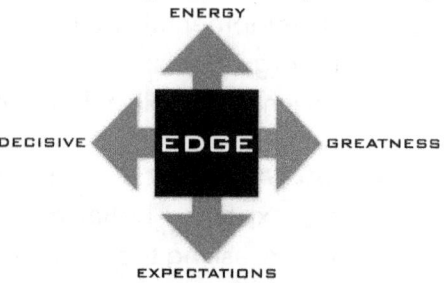

Today, change your focus to put coaching first. Make it your priority, and your team's behaviors will change, and so will your results.

12 | COMPLACENCY IS THE ENEMY OF LONGEVITY

Longevity, Tenure, Seniority… businesses today value these things. In the current world of Generation X, Y, Z, etc., it is getting harder and harder to imagine an employee sticking around for more than a couple of years.

Longevity with a company brings many valued things. It provides confidence, competence, and historical knowledge of what works and what doesn't. It allows someone the potential ability to become a teacher, mentor, or coach for the other "newbies" to the company. These are the veterans we come to rely on when the going gets tough. These are the ones who know how to put out small fires before they become big ones.

One of the goals of an organization is to build a team of talented, experienced team members who don't have to be micromanaged in order to get the job done. This is how the proverbial "well-oiled machine" is formed.

The only chink in the armor of longevity is the potential for complacency. When people feel comfortable in their roles, they often don't feel challenged. Thinking outside the box becomes unnecessary. Remembering and following the rulebook fades into a set of "unofficial best practices or quick steps." These simplified methods can work if they are intentionally designed with policies and procedures kept in mind, but the danger lies in circumventing the proper steps in favor of speed.

Complacency allows leaders to sit back and accept things. It allows them to procrastinate, putting off until tomorrow the things that should be done today. It creates the feeling, "It'll be ok, don't worry about it." It prevents people from taking action.

Complacency also stifles creativity and innovation. It is the feeling that the old way of doing things is best. It makes one feel that their ideas and suggestions won't be welcomed or valued and drives down the level on the Commitment Ladder to a level around grudging compliance.

The worst thing about complacency in a leader is that it breeds more complacency in his or her team.

Desiring a team of strong, tenured leaders with high longevity is good. Desiring tenured leaders who develop fresh ideas and raise the performance bar is even better.

Challenge your team to continue to strive to be the best. Challenge them to throw complacency out the window and accept nothing less than reaching their goals. Don't allow procrastination or surrendering to "doing things the way they've always been done." These things create complacency.

A winning leader committed to the organization's objectives supports the vision but challenges the norm. They don't accept incomplete results. They constantly raise the "standards bar" for themselves and for their team.

Longevity gives a leader a strong foundation to stand on while looking at their team's performance. Challenging complacency drives them to climb even higher.

13 | CONFIDENCE AND COMPETENCE

I was watching my son play the guitar the other day. He is just amazing at it. He and his band play shows at a local club where the kids from our city like to hang out. He plays guitar, bass, violin, sings, and tries his hand at the drums. (He's very talented if you don't mind a little bragging from a proud dad.)

But his amazing sound wasn't always very amazing. I still have nightmares about the days when he first picked up the guitar. You might think I'm joking...believe me, I'm not. It was complete torture. The screeching, the wrong notes...aaauggg! In fact, I can never enjoy *"Sweet Child O' Mine"* by Guns n' Roses again!

But...he practiced. He received a few lessons. And... He got better. And that's when it happened. As soon as he started to improve, his confidence level grew. And that's when he REALLY started to improve. It took a long time to learn that first song, but once he did, it took half the time to learn the next one. And once he learned that one, it took half the time to learn the next one, and so on. Pretty soon, he would hear a song once or twice, read the sheet music, and play it immediately.

His confidence continued to grow and grow. Pretty soon, he didn't even really need to read the notes; he could "play it by ear." And that's when it happened. He began writing his own songs. He started just writing small parts and solos, then morphed into full songs. He has now written around fifteen complete songs and recorded seven.

By the way, did I mention that he is only 16 years old?

I'm not sharing all this just to dote on my son. I'm sharing it to convey the power that *competence* and *confidence have* on performance.

Closing the Knowledge Gap fully means that you provide *knowledge* through training and teaching. But it also means that you develop *skills* as well, and the only way to do that is to practice.

Winning leaders ensure that they build their teams' confidence by building their competence. They practice and practice with their teams until they get them to the point of competence. This is where the leaders validate that they can perform to the expected levels and achieve the expected results.

The winning leaders know that the Knowledge Gap is closed once the team members perform to this expectation level and achieve the expected results.

The beauty of this is that competence leads to confidence, and then confidence leads to a higher level of competence.

Just think about something you learned and are now competent and confident in. Riding a bike, typing, driving a car...many of these things you probably do so competently and with such confidence that you don't even think about the motions your body is taking. They just happen.

Wouldn't it be fantastic if your team performed the same way? Imagine your team members performing so effectively that they don't have to think about it. It just becomes a natural part of who they are. Wow! It happens for winning leaders.

You can get there. It just takes a tremendous amount of focus and discipline on your part. Winning leaders understand this and put out the effort to ensure their team members have both the knowledge and the skills to be competent in their jobs. They then provide support and recognition to reinforce the behaviors...which all lead to confidence.

It takes a lot of effort to learn to play beautiful music. Along the way, your team members may hit some sour notes and may want to quit practicing. But, with a winning leader behind them, the competence levels will soon grow, and then the confidence levels will grow. And soon, you will be playing beautiful music together!

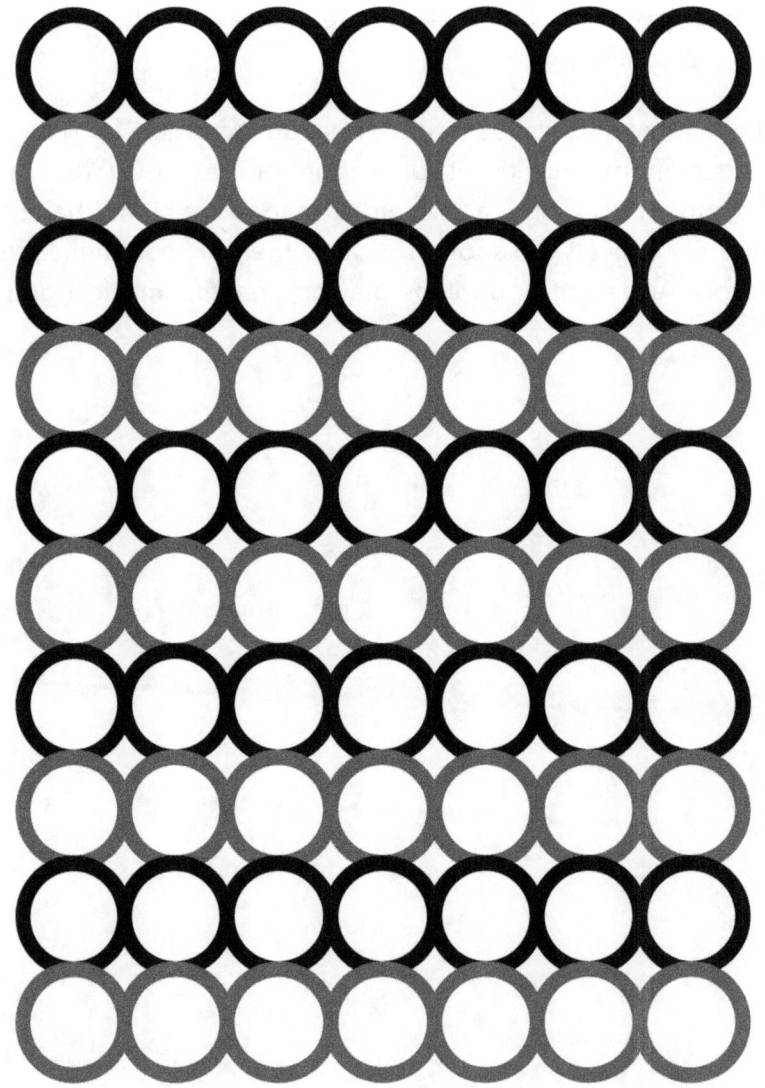

14 | CULTURE

What do you think of when you hear the word "Culture?"

Do you imagine the high-society type wearing Chanel haute couture and sipping tea in his or her castle? Or you could picture a more anthropological view, reflecting on the historical cultures of the Central American Mayans or Australian Aborigines.

Whatever your natural view of culture, one thing bonds together the many uses of the word. The collective similarities shared between the core individuals in a society create the culture.

How is this culture created?

Culture is created when all parties living within that society hold an overwhelming belief in a system of actions. Leaders create the culture of their organization both intentionally and unintentionally.

Winning leaders understand this, and they leverage their ability to create a winning culture. They know their team members, talk to them, and ask questions. They set clear objectives and expectations. They train and create importance around what actions are expected. They measure results and provide coaching, counseling, and recognition for each team member's performance. They know how to relax and have fun in an environment of success. They create a shared vision amongst the team. *They care.*

Cultures are created whether we intend them to or not. When team members are ignored, a culture of discourse is created. A culture of intolerance is created when team members are verbally or emotionally abused, when a leader stops caring, a culture of apathy and non-compliance results.

However, when a leader challenges team members to exceed expectations, a culture of winning is created. When they are recognized and rewarded, a culture of celebration is created. When they are coached to perform at a higher level, a culture of teaching is created.

Winning leaders apply these ideals to everything they do. They know that their words and their actions will create the culture in which they live. They embrace this responsibility and live it in each moment that they lead.

Leaders create culture. Gapology creates a culture of action. A culture of action creates a culture of winning. What culture will you create?

15 | DANDELIONS

Don't you just hate dandelions? I sure do.

It seems as though one day, my lawn is a luscious green carpet, mowed, trimmed, watered, fed, and perfectly manicured into something the neighbors drool over, but then the next morning, I woke up, and it had ten million dandelions all over it! I try and try and try to eliminate them, but they always keep coming back. Why are they so pervasive?

That's when it hit me...they have a backup plan. The flower heads mature to contain hundreds of little seeds with a little fluffy white parachute attached so that when the wind blows, they are carried throughout the yard.

I can fertilize, spray, and pull them until my thumb *literally* turns green, but in the end, they win. They always win.

This method of having a backup plan, or in our case, a succession plan, would also benefit leaders. Just as eliminating 1 or 2 individual dandelions has no effect on the dandelions' overall succession plans, having a plan for your team would provide a strong defense against any of your team members' departures.

But all plans, succession or otherwise, require a winning leader who ensures that his or her team is always staffed with Talent. These plans need the type of leader who identifies the needs, sets clear behavioral and result expectations, measures results, manages Performance Gaps and provides effective consequences and recognition. The leader must understand the emotional temperature of the team members and quickly identify those who may potentially leave for other opportunities. The leader must be proactive. The leader must *prepare* for the vacancy.

Winning leaders prepare by sourcing candidates even when they don't need them. They start building a network of relationships early to have a list of people they can contact when the openings happen.

This prevents the "warm blood" syndrome. This means that when an opening happens that a leader is not prepared for, the sense of urgency skyrockets, and the temptation to hire anyone who simply has a heartbeat grows. Just getting someone, anyone, hired is the driving force for this leader. With this, the wrong person for the job is often hired, and then huge problems seem to happen (which eventually create another opening!).

It is always better not to hire someone than to hire the wrong person! It costs less, both financially and emotionally!

So, how do you develop a succession plan? Here are seven successful steps that others have used in the past:

1. ***Determine the qualifications*** (What Competency and Commitment level is expected, and where on your team's *"ABC Ranking"* is this person expected to fit. Will they be a "Star Player"? Will they be just "Acceptable"?)

2. ***Understand the needs*** (Now and future).

3. ***Determine who will do the recruiting.*** (Who is good at it, and who can be mentored for development?)

4. **Schedule it** (Set hard dates AND times).

5. **Do it**! (Get out there! Empower your team to support your efforts)

6. **Scorecard it** (Who, what, where, and when is tracked, and then results are measured and action taken based on the results)

7. **Report it** (Let the team and your supervisor know the results. This creates a sense of team in the mission to have a full staff 100% of the time, and it sets a level of accountability and partnership with your supervisor.)

Use the planning strategy of the dandelion. Understand that it KNOWS that it's going to get eliminated. It knows it must have a succession plan to protect its future. Each dandelion creates many seeds. Is *your* succession planning strategy that strong?

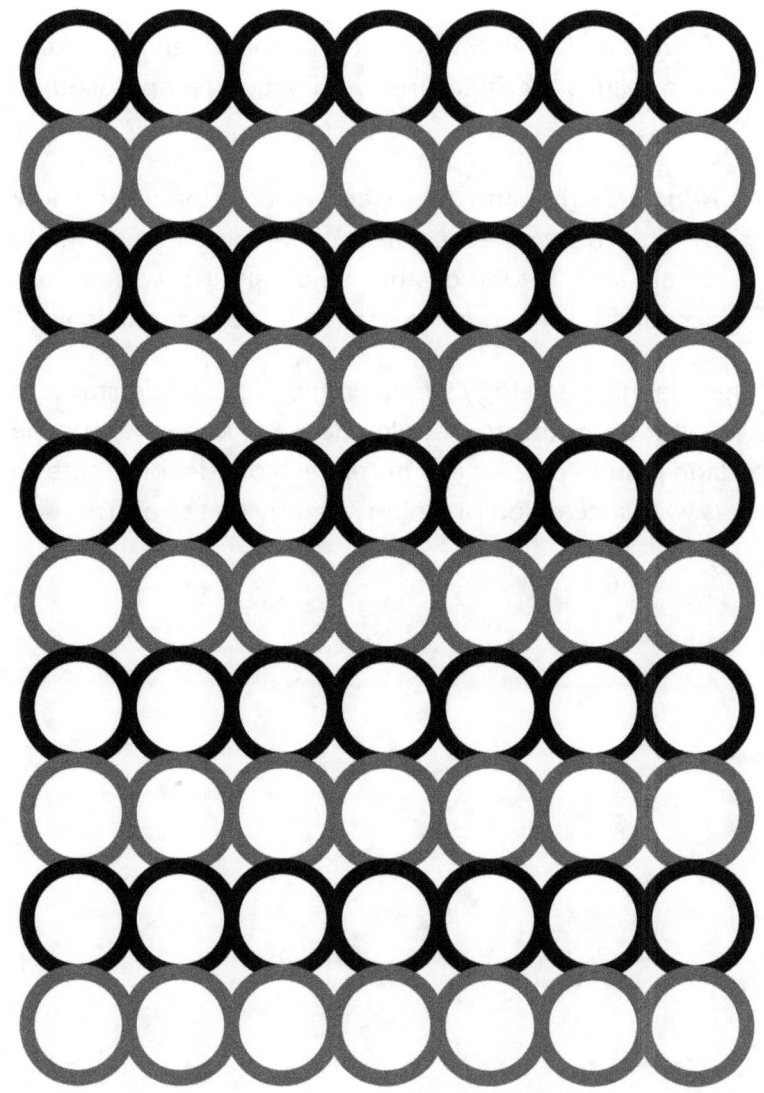

16 | DECATHLON

"Life is a marathon, not a sprint."

Leaders who inspire people to live life at a slow but steady pace and avoid taking the quick and easy approach to things have used this quote for years. Its message is that we must work hard daily, be patient, and follow the plan to achieve our goals.

Much of this is true, but life, particularly winning leadership, is more like the decathlon than the marathon alone.

The decathlon is a track and field sporting event that takes place over a period of two days and consists of performing ten different events. On the first day, the athletes compete in the 100-meter dash, long jump, shot put, high jump, and 400-meter dash. On the second day, they take on the 110-meter hurdles, discus, pole vault, javelin, and 1500-meter run.

This decathlon winner is typically crowned the "World's Greatest Athlete." Still, the interesting thing about this event is that the winner may not win many of the individual races or competitions. But...he or she must consistently be a top performer in almost every event.

One of the obstacles these athletes face is that as they focus on training for one event, their skills in another are diminished because of the time needed to be dedicated to each event. For instance, while one person runs mile after mile to get in shape for the 1500-meter race, another athlete is lifting weights to build muscles for the shot put.

For someone to be crowned the "World's Greatest Athlete," they must focus their preparation on all the events and develop their overall skills to the highest levels possible.

This is not unlike the challenge for winning leaders. Our teams face many challenges that we must help them overcome. Sometimes, they must react quickly; sometimes, they must hurdle over problems; sometimes, they must lift heavy burdens and cast them aside; and sometimes, they must give their best effort for the long haul.

As we go through our days, weeks, and years as leaders of others, we need to understand that we must be constantly training in all areas of our business. We need to be flexible and understand our own athletes' needs. What Knowledge Gaps can we close with them? What Importance Gaps can we close with them? Do they need to work on their selling or service skills? Do they need to work on their interpersonal relationship skills? How about time management or analytical skills?

Understanding that people have two or three inherent strengths that can be leveraged to compensate for the weaker ones, the winning leader will continue cross-training his or her team members to strengthen their overall skill sets. By doing this, the leader creates talent and improves the overall mindset of their team.

Think about all the many things we ask them to do. We expect them to be great at everything. We demand it from them. We set clear behavioral and result expectations for them. We hold them accountable. We measure their results in all the areas and then reward or create consequences for their performance.

As coaches, we need to understand the many different expectations and understand how to best help our teams balance their training so that we set them up for success when they are released to the public. We need to close any Knowledge or Importance Gaps they have. We need to know what areas they are confident and competent in and what areas need our direction or support. It is up to us to coach, lead, and motivate them so that when the time comes to compete for us, they will be physically, mentally, and emotionally ready to move to Action.

"Life is a decathlon, not a sprint." Once we live the life of a performance coach, our teams will perform…no matter how many "events" we expect them to compete in!

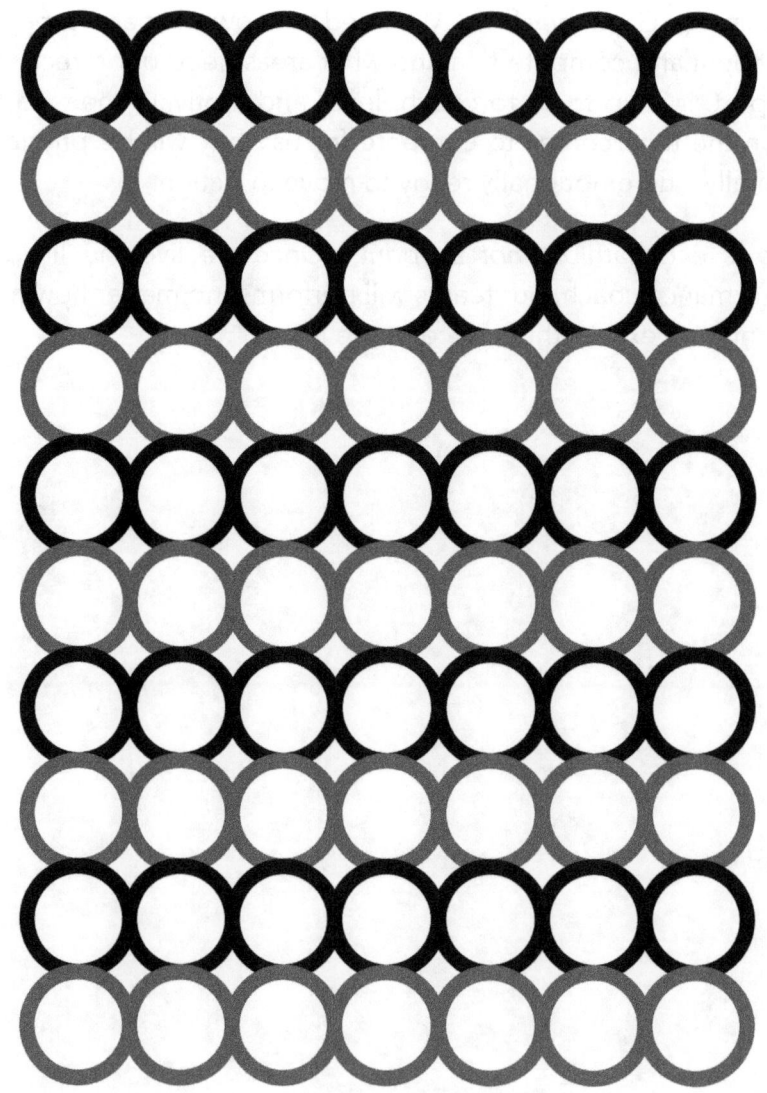

17 | DIAMOND IN THE ROUGH

"Diamonds are a girl's best friend."

Many people are very familiar with this Marilyn Monroe quote. I'm not sure I get it. I mean, well, it's just a little, sparkly, clear rock. What's the big deal? Plus, the fact that it costs more than a flat-screen TV, my son's used pickup truck, and a case of Bud Light combined. Maybe men really are from Mars.

I must admit it, though…diamonds are beautiful. But…they don't begin their lives as things of beauty.

They start out as ordinary carbon-bearing materials. They could easily end up as plain old, boring graphite or coal, but because of the right amount of heat and pressure delivered by the weight of the earth or a crashing meteor, the carbon transforms into one of the most treasured objects on earth.

This is not unlike the members of our teams. Many of them are valuable, yet few of them we initially identify as a "Diamond in the Rough."

What winning leaders suggest, however, is that we dig deeper. Every single one of our team members is a true "Diamond in the Rough," and their shiny value may come from simple things.

For example, they may enjoy talking to people. You see them easily approach customers to talk to them about the weather, their outfits, or their hair. They seem bubbly and outgoing. This is one reason why you hired them!

But...they struggle with the idea of suggesting products or services. They cringe at the thought of selling. Their easy-going demeanor quickly vanishes when they must talk about something outside their comfort zone.

These are your "Diamonds in the Rough." A winning leader sees through the dirt and grime and creates the three "C's." (No, not Color, Cut, and Clarity) They give them Confidence, Competence and help them to become Committed.

Diamonds in the Rough can be discovered in every area of our business. We need to look for them. They may be a commissioned, salaried, or even hourly associate. They may not even be aware of their own sparkle; it is up to the winning leader to spot it.

Do you have an associate who is eager to help you with a task? Or do you have a manager who is always reading leadership books?

These are your diamonds. You already own them. They are within your reach.

Take the time and take the actions necessary to give them what they need so they won't become an ordinary lump of coal.

Give them training and teach them using skill-building activities that are designed for the adult learner, provide clear results and behavioral expectations, measure their progress, and provide recognition and coaching to give them the momentum to keep going.

This is how you create your own diamonds. This is how you give them Confidence, Competence, and Commitment.

And speaking of commitment, remember this quote from the De Beers Company, *"A Diamond is Forever."*

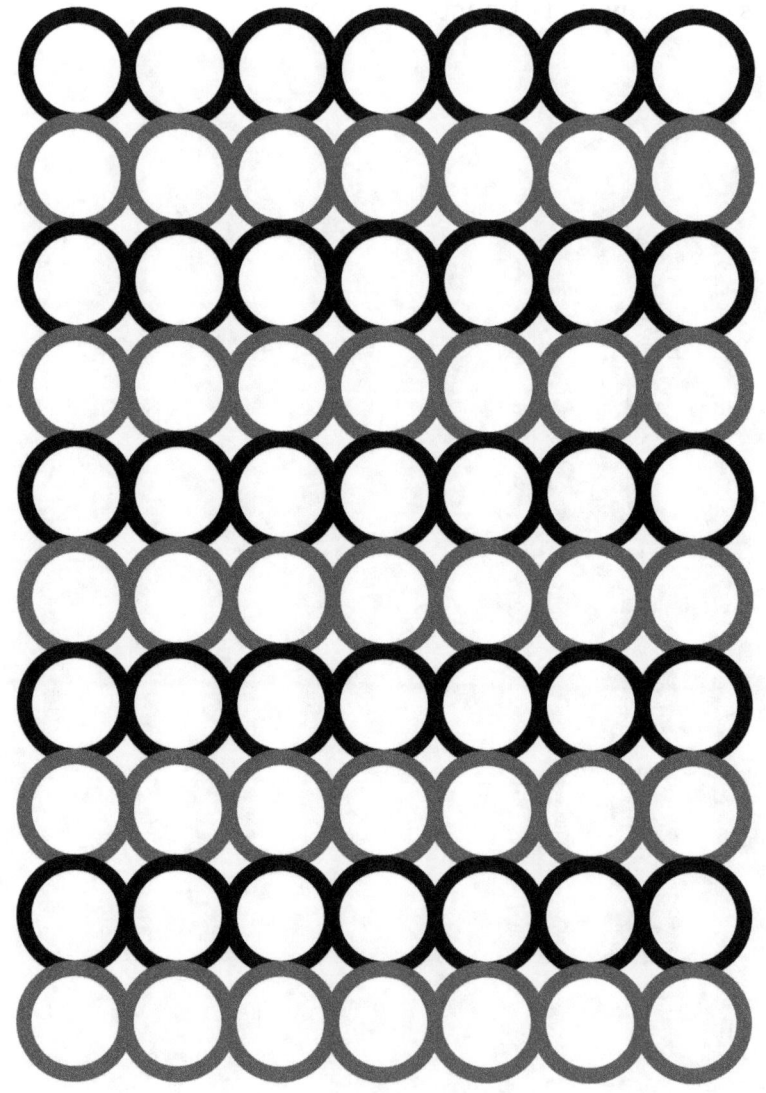

18 | ENCORE...ENCORE...

Have you ever wondered what it would be like to be a rock star? Just imagine it. Picture yourself walking out onto that stage, staring into the faces of everyone who came to see you. Imagine them screaming your name. Imagine them jumping up and down and dancing to your songs. Imagine them going crazy when you walk out for your encore.

How do you think you'd feel? How would their screams and cheers impact your performance? Would you want to perform again the next night?

For most artists, this is what drives them. They get to do something they are passionate about, get paid for it, and then get the huge high created by a roaring crowd. This is what creates the momentum for them. It's what they live for.

Winning leaders create a similar environment for their teams.

When an associate meets an expectation, the leader goes crazy. They make the associate feel like a rock star. One-on-one, they personally look them in the eye and shake their hand. They tell them specifically how much they appreciate what they've accomplished. They showed interest in the process the associate followed to achieve the results by asking specific questions about the steps involved. They thank them by making the achievement important.

And then the celebration starts. Once the personal recognition is complete, they publicly thank them. They post the results. They ensure that everyone, perhaps even the customers, knows what a special accomplishment was achieved. They get everyone else in on the action by creating a standing ovation and making sure that the day isn't just another ordinary day...it is a special day.

Winning leaders know their team members and understand who responds to this type of recognition, and they leverage that information. Occasionally, team members may be a bit shy regarding public recognition, so they set the tone for recognizing them at the appropriate level. But for the rest, the world is a stage, and the leader is the audience who showers praise on those who meet and exceed their expectations.

The results created from loud, foot-stomping recognition are amazing. Lives change. Performances change. Results change. Commitment levels change.

In our world, "thanks" has become too commonplace. We hear it all the time. It is becoming a casual word just thrown around without much feeling behind it. We see it in everyone from cashiers to mechanics to teachers. Everyone throws out that word without even looking the other person in the eye. It has lost its meaning and the power behind it. Starting today, stop and think about that word. Does "thanks" really mean *Thank YOU?*" Does the impact of the word match your feelings? Does it match the level of accomplishment? Does it change lives?

Winning leaders change lives and results by leveraging these powerful words. They make them important. They do so because they understand that while the results are important, even more important are the rock stars that achieve them! Thank YOU!

19 | FAMILY

What is family? You may think about love, respect, support, friendly competition, and community.

I was looking at the TV Guide list of the top 10 television shows of all time, and guess what? 6 of them are about families… Most of them were a bit dysfunctional…

- I Love Lucy

- The Honeymooners

- All in the Family

- The Sopranos

- The Simpsons

- The Andy Griffith Show

In looking at these, I don't see a lot of commonalities with the families in the real world. There is no way that these fictional characters are anything like us.

Lucy and Ralph Cramden were crazy and always up to some crazy scheme. Archie and Edith Bunker were always arguing. Tony Soprano was depressed and saw a psychiatrist. Homer eats donuts, drinks beer, and watches TV; Andy Griffith had a best friend who was sweet but completely nuts.

See, these characters are nothing like us! Well... maybe a little. (It's a good thing that they don't make a sitcom about my life, that's for sure!)

Winning leaders build a culture of family. They develop a team that values and supports each other. It is one that encourages and challenges each other. It is one that has a common objective, which is to win by leveraging the strengths and talents of each member in a culture of positivity.

As leaders, we must discover and understand the relationships that occur in our teams. While fighting against naturally occurring relationships is tempting, open-minded people embrace them and help nurture them into healthy, positive ones focused on common objectives and expectations.

When people work together as closely as we do in our teams, it is natural that our team members will bond and form friendships. It's also natural that they may disagree or get annoyed occasionally. But a winning leader provides his or her team with a common vision that is motivating and inspirational. This inspiration is what creates commitment and motivation, which leads the team to win. Win as an organization, win as a team, and win as a family.

At times can we be a bit dysfunctional? Sure, but when the credits roll on our own daily episodes, we always end up together, usually laughing, having survived another winning day.

Maybe Homer and I have more in common than I thought...

20 | FEEL THE FIRE

A term I recently heard from a winning restaurant industry leader hit home with me. He was talking about "Feeling the Fire."

Something he frequently does on visits to his locations is get actively involved in the kitchen. He jumps right behind the grill and experiences what his team of chefs goes through each day. He says there is no better way to know your people and learn what motivates them or causes Gaps than living some time in their shoes and feeling the same fire they feel every day.

In Gapology, we call this "Living the Being Level."

On the Knowing-Doing-Being scale, we describe what it means to move team members from a *"Knowing"* level (where they have a solid understanding of what

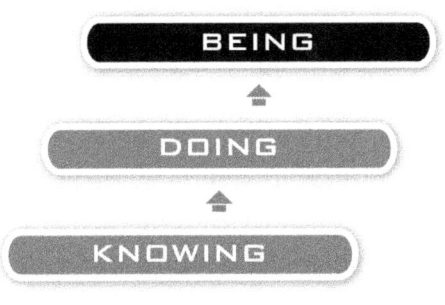

is expected) to a *"Doing"* level (where they have the skills to be able to demonstrate the behavioral expectations) to the *"Being"* level (where the team members have a total commitment and belief in the expectations). Once at the "Being" level, the team members live the behaviors, meet the result expectations consistently, and build a culture around winning in that particular expectation. In fact, at this level, teaching and inspiring others has become the culture.

Winning leaders live at this "Being" level in all areas that drive their most important metrics and initiatives. They understand what specific behaviors dramatically impact their results, and then they move themselves and their teams from Knowing to Doing and finally to Being in these behaviors.

Feeling the Fire is the first step in that process. The winning leader understands that to be effective, they must understand completely what their team experiences. They must understand it firsthand. They cannot just read about or observe it; they must live it. They know that they don't have to do it daily, but they also know that many Knowledge Gaps are created when they assume they understand what their teams do.

When I hear the old term "Leading by Example," I reflect on the difference between this method of "Feeling the Fire." Many new leaders struggle with understanding the difference between doing the work themselves and truly being an example of the expected behaviors. They tend to do the work without reflecting on what's working and what's not. They tend to do it and not give direction or coaching while they work. They just become part of the team.

While showing our team that we want to feel the fire to learn and grow as a leader and demonstrate that we are willing to do anything we ask of them is a positive message to send; staying in that role limits our ability to lead. Winning leaders jump in to learn and help when necessary but don't remain there. They look for Gaps, determine fresher, better ways of doing things, and coach and mentor "in the moment." They are not just a worker but a real leader who is leading by example.

Winning leaders understand their teams and roles intimately and can train, teach, and inspire them at a moment's notice. They don't lead from afar. Even if the leader is three states away from one of their team members, they know the business so well that they can ask pointed questions over the phone that uncover Gaps and special needs that the team may have. They ask questions like, "What are you working on?" "Why are you working on that?" "Where are you in the process?" "When do you expect to be done with it?" and "How can I help you?"

Open-ended questions like these uncover what is happening in the team member's world, and because the leader has felt the fire, they have a deep understanding of what it is like in their daily life. With this knowledge and experience, they can better provide the right amount of direction and support.

Winning leaders understand what makes each team member tick, what motivates them, what Gaps they have, and what help they need. They do so because they understand what it is like to live in their shoes. They do so because they "Feel the Fire."

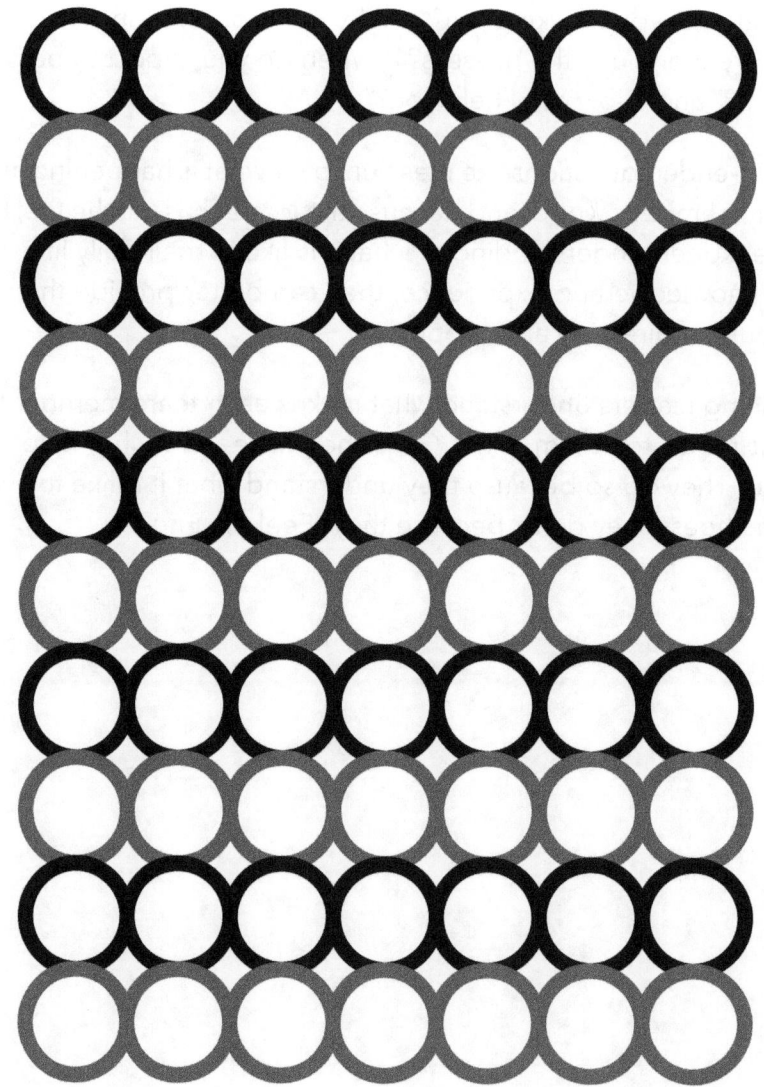

21 | FILTERS

Thank goodness for the atmosphere. It is the atmosphere of the Earth that makes life possible. Along with retaining heat on our surface, it also filters out deadly radiation from the sun. Without this filter, our beautiful planet would be unlivable, not to mention...we'd have one heck of a sunburn.

Filters in communication, however, have the potential to make leadership unlivable.

When looking at any ordinary organizational chart, we may not immediately see the filters, but they are there, living in the minds and hearts of each team member—these filters scatter or block elements of any message being delivered by the leader who is sending it.

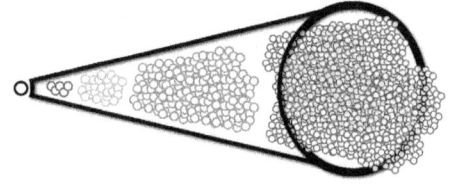

In this diagram, you'll see that a message sent by a single leader that flows out to many team members is impacted by the outer rim of each tiny circle. Picture this as the filter we refer to and imagine how the leader's message can evolve.

These filters are created by the receiver's focus, level of interest, prejudices, past experiences, and many other distractions. These filters impact the level of importance that the receiver feels about the topic and directly impact what is being absorbed, understood, believed in, and acted upon.

Every level and every team member has a filter, and every leader must learn how to ensure that the critical elements of their messages are passed through the filter to the parties who must understand the messages, understand their importance, and understand that they must take action around them.

Winning leaders have learned that clarity, simplicity, and alignment are the secrets to delivering filter-proof messages.

- Communication must be clear. There must be no mistake about what the message is, what the expectations are, what priority levels are, and who owns the action. Winning leaders explain what needs to be done, how it needs to be done, why it needs to be done, when it needs to be done, and who needs to do it. This clarity creates commitment to the message by eliminating any questions or doubts.

- Communication must be simple. When simple messages around the most important things that must be done are clouded with many other less important things, team members won't understand the priorities and expectations. When we state that "A" is the most important thing but then layer in "B, C, D, E, and F," "A" gets lost in the shuffle. Winning leaders focus their message on "A." They talk about it first, last, and most often. They don't allow "B, C, D, E, and F" to scatter the focus from "A."

- Communication must create alignment. A simple, clear message that is delivered to create a shared vision around the top priorities and expectations develops a team of committed, focused team members who are willing to stand up for and act upon what they believe is right. This team that is focused on the most important things won't be distracted or swayed from achieving their expectations. They believe in them. They live for them. They will do anything to achieve them.

Winning leaders understand that filters exist. They know that there is nothing they can do to remove them. But they also know that they can work with them by acknowledging their existence. They create a leadership rhythm that their teams count on. They are simple and direct in their message around expectations and accountability. They are clear and precise with their process of training and teaching. They are committed to developing a culture of specific priorities around the things that truly make a difference and filter out the distractions before they even begin to send the messages.

Winning leaders also understand that each team member will filter out the pieces of the message that they feel are unimportant or don't pertain to them. They will block out the things that don't impact their world directly. Their filter creates their internal priority list. As leaders, it is up to them to hit the point about what is essential to winning on their team. They do this with clear, simple communication that creates alignment around expectations.

Winning leaders also understand that they do this with their actions. They know that they communicate in non-verbal ways that can either contradict or reinforce what they say verbally. The things that they say are the most important must be the things that they follow up on, create accountability around, and celebrate. They know that their actions must match their words, and their words *must* pass through the filters to prevent and close any Performance Gaps within their teams.

Now, where is that sunscreen?

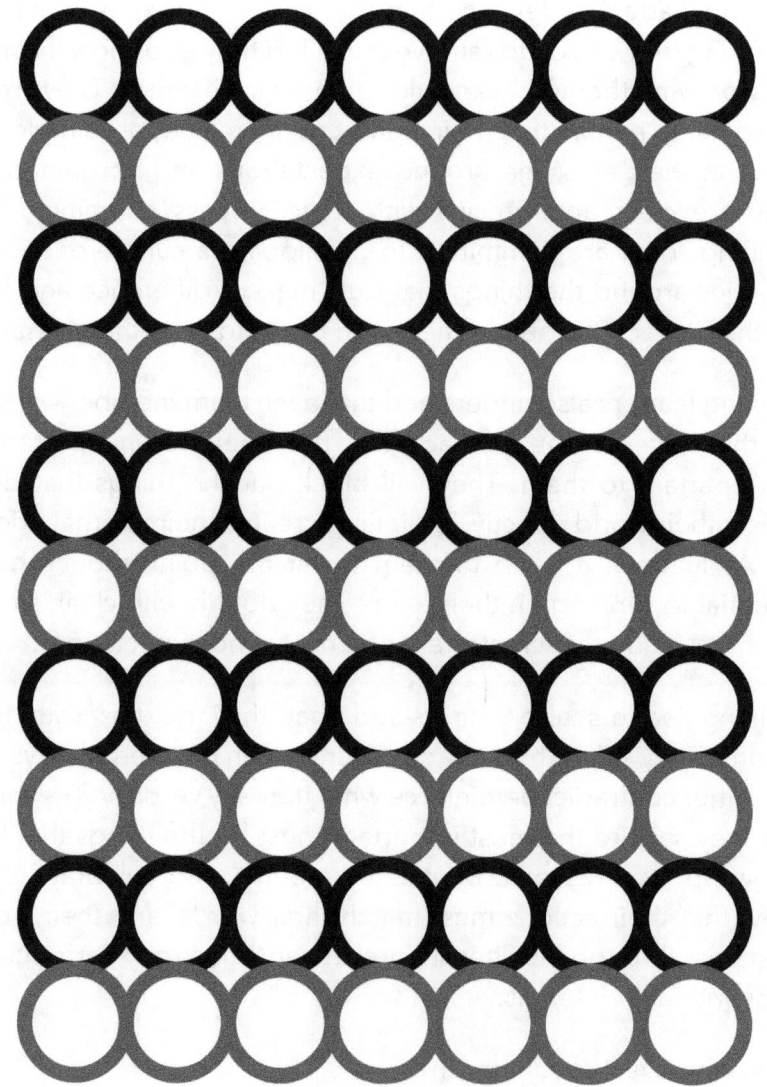

22 | GOALS AND EXPECTATIONS

There is always a lot of talk about goals in the business world. "SMART" goals (Specific, Measurable, Achievable, Relevant, and Time-based) are one of the extremely valuable tools companies use in their development processes. Goals are important to have. Short-term goals give us motivation. Long-term goals give us vision. If we didn't have goals in our lives, it would be very difficult to achieve the things we desire.

One thing we need to ensure, however, is that we don't get goals confused with expectations.

Think about the term "goal." A goal is usually something distant that you hope to achieve.

Now, think about the term "expectation." Think about what it means to "expect" something.

Expecting something means that you KNOW it is going to happen. There is no doubt. You go through your daily life feeling convinced that the result will occur.

It's like throwing a ball into the air. You know it will fall back down...you are convinced it will...you EXPECT it will.

When leading a team, they must understand your desires and objectives. Do they know what your goals are and what your expectations are? Do they know that expectations MUST be delivered? Do they know that you expect nothing less?

Are you as shocked when one of your team members' expectations isn't met as you would be if you threw the ball into the air and it didn't come back down?

Your team's behaviors will directly reflect how you manage your expectations. When they aren't met, and you don't react, they won't react either. When they aren't met, and you do react, they will react as well.

Expectations to be met need to have two elements clearly defined.

- The first element is *Behavioral Expectation*. These are the <u>actions</u> you expect to see in your team members.

- The second element is the *Result Expectation*. This is the <u>outcome</u> you expect to see based on the team member performing the Behavioral Expectation.

A leader often provides only one of the two expectations and creates Importance and Action Gaps. If the Behavioral Expectation is only provided, the associate won't know the desired outcome and, therefore, won't understand the true importance of their actions. If the Result Expectation is only provided, the associate won't understand the exact steps they must take to reach the desired outcome.

Winning leaders understand that we must be very clear with both elements when laying out our expectations if we "EXPECT" them to be delivered. What do you expect?

23 | GOOD LUCK

Winning the lottery is luck. Winning at Bingo is luck. Winning in real life, especially in leadership...is definitely not luck.

An old saying from American Motors CEO Roy D. Chapin Jr. goes, "Be ready when the opportunity comes. Luck is the time when preparation and opportunity meet."

Looking at many of the famous rock stars over the years, very few achieved their stardom from luck alone. The vast majority worked hard at it for years and years. They practiced with second-hand equipment in their garages and basements and fought with the neighbors about "all that racket." They argued with bandmates about lyrics or notes and struggled to create songs they would love to play and that their fans would love to hear. But in the end, all this hard work and practice time paid off. It paid off, not because they were "lucky" or got a "lucky break," but instead, it paid off because they were prepared when the right producer or agent heard them.

They were prepared for the opportunity.

As winning leaders, we cannot wait to be lucky. We cannot sit on our current performance and wait for the customers to come to our doors or for our bosses to recognize us.

We need to prepare.

We must look at specific behaviors needed to win...and then prepare our teams to execute them. We need to close and prevent any Knowledge Gaps for them. They need to know what to do and how to do it. We must provide them with the knowledge to perform specific behaviors. Then, we need to practice with them until they have the skill to perform to the level of expectation that will consistently achieve the desired results.

We then need to prepare them with the inspiration to win by ensuring that all Importance Gaps are closed for our team. They need to understand why the specific behaviors need to be performed. They need to feel it in their bones. They must believe in it so much that they would never dream of "not executing" the behaviors. We also need to help them understand where in their priority list the behaviors fall. They should know that these behaviors are the most important things they are responsible for, and nothing must come before them.

Helping them to prioritize will lead them through the whirlwind of daily tasks by providing a clear level of importance around the specific things that will help them win.

And finally, we need them to act. Our teams need to perform the specific behaviors they've been preparing for. They need to take the steps leading them toward the expected results. And while they are acting, we must act as well. We must coach them along the way. If they get off track, we need to be there to redirect them. If they stay on track, we need to be there to reward them. These leadership behaviors of coaching and recognition will build strong, motivating momentum to continue moving the overall team toward positive results and winning performance.

Our competitors and peers will then step back and wonder, "How did he/she get so lucky to have such great results?"

We will know, however, that luck had nothing to do with it. Our "luck" was just the result of our preparation and opportunity. We worked through the preparation and created the opportunity.

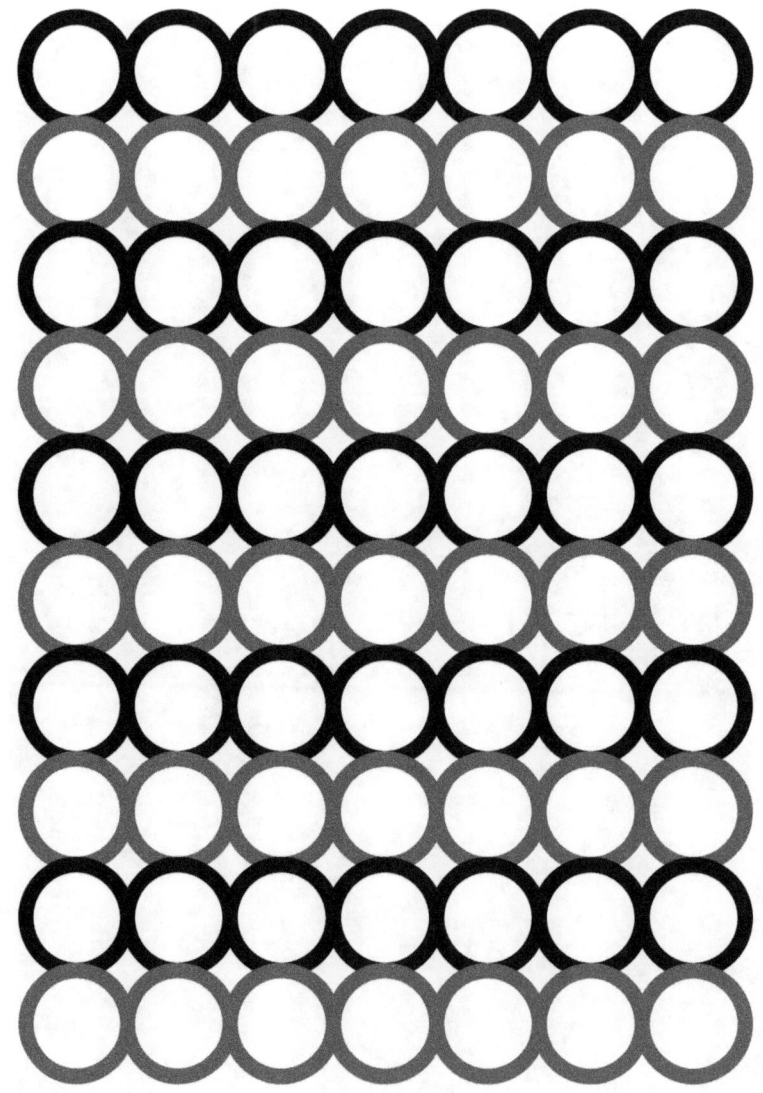

24 | GOOD TIMES AND BAD TIMES

John C. Maxwell says in his book, *The Right to Lead,* "Leadership is often easy during the good times. It's when everything seems to be against you - when you're out of energy and you don't want to lead - that you earn your place as a leader. During every season of life, leaders face crucial moments when they must choose between gearing up or giving up. To make it through those times, rely on the rock of discipline, not the shifting sand of emotion."[2]

When I think of the most famous leaders throughout history, I think of people like George Washington, Martin Luther King, Franklin Delano Roosevelt, and Susan B. Anthony.

A common thread for these leaders is that none came into notoriety during this country's good times. They became signature leaders because of their strength and vision during times of struggle. They were relied upon for their bravery, focus, and commitment to achieving nothing but the ultimate goals they set for themselves, their country, and the world around them.

I know that leading our teams may not be the same as leading a country through a Revolution, Civil Rights movement, World War, or Women's Rights movement, but the concepts required to

---

[2] Maxwell, John C. <u>The Right to Lead</u>. Thomas Nelson, 2010.

succeed are the same. Crucial moments impact the lives of our team members and customers and require tough decision-making or challenging conversations. Situations like coaching, counseling, apologizing, or even asking for help may create feelings of stress and anxiety. They may also make you want to avoid the situation altogether.

But...these are the times when true winning leadership is needed. This is where E.D.G.E. (Energy, Decisiveness, Greatness, and Expectations) is needed. Winning leaders are the compasses that teams follow to the land of greener pastures. They are the North Star that teams use to guide their ships to the New World.

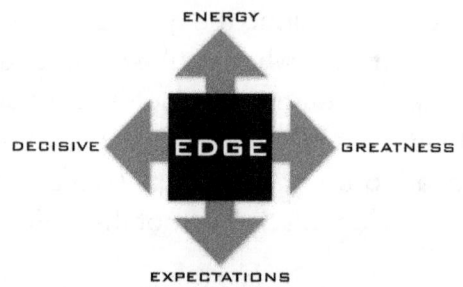

As winning leaders, we must clearly define what must happen for our businesses to succeed. We must be disciplined in our leadership to provide that clear vision to our teams. We also must avoid making tough decisions from a place of strong emotion. Winning leaders stop, breathe, and think before reacting to tough situations. They know that good decisions come from a place of calm.

So today, take a minute and reflect on the tremendous strength of will that it took for leaders like the ones mentioned above to make their significant impact in the world. Reflect on their undying focus and devotion to their cause. Think about how hard it must have been for them to fight the good fight in the face of tremendous adversity. It would have been very easy for them to quit and walk away. Their lives would have been a lot simpler, that is for sure...but would the world be the same? Fight the good fight...Make a difference in the world around you!

25 | HEART POWER

Thousands, perhaps millions, of poems, songs, and stories have been written about the human heart over the years. "Why?" This is the question I want to explore.

After all, the heart is simply an organ in the body of any creature with a circulatory system. In humans, it begins beating at around five weeks and beats approximately 2.5 billion times during an average 66-year lifespan. Its job is to collect de-oxygenated blood from the body's veins, send it through the lungs to exchange carbon dioxide for oxygen, and then return it to the body through a series of arteries. Simple...right?

Well, that's one way to look at the heart. The other way is a bit more philosophical. In this sense, the heart contains the spirit and drives our actions. The heart is what moves us to care and to hate. It has been the cause of more wars than we can name, but it has also driven such outstanding examples of generosity and giving that it has become the very symbol of love.

It is what creates passion.

In the business world that we all live in, we must understand this metaphysical heart. The heart that drives us to do the things we do.

This heart power is stronger than any other force we experience. It compels us to act or not to act. It compels us to win or to lose. It pushes us to overcome obstacles or collapse before them. It lifts us to higher heights or smothers us beneath its weight.

Winning leaders tap into this power to close Importance and Action Gaps. They figure out ways to generate, build, and leverage it. They seek new methods of understanding how the heart drives each team member. They listen for the beating of their hearts and respond with their own passionate motivation when the beats are too slow. They provide a necessary calm when the beats become too fast from tough situations. They understand that they must become the electrical current that controls the beats of the team.

Winning leaders understand all this and that anything is possible with a team of passionate players whose hearts are all beating in time.

Leaders throughout the centuries have built their kingdoms through the hearts of soldiers willing to sacrifice themselves for the greater cause. The heart is the reason for many scientific and human discoveries. General relativity, the universe's expansion, planetary rotation, germ theory, penicillin, and insulin were all discovered by people who were driven by their hearts to learn the secrets of the scientific world.

Reach out to your team members. Discover what moves their hearts. Understand it, embrace it, and touch it. Where you move their spirits and hearts, so will you move their hands and minds.

26 | HORSE TO WATER

"You can lead a horse to water, but you can't make it drink."

The same thing goes for any team members...well, perhaps the saying would be more appropriate if it read: "You can lead a team member to the point of action, but it is up to them to act."

As a leader, you can give your associates everything they need to succeed. You can hire a quality person who comes to you with transferable skills and provide them with quality training that delivers knowledge and builds their skills. You can set clear expectations that lay out the expected behaviors and the expected results. You can lead them to understand why something is important and when it needs to be done. You can even provide motivation and inspiration through a process of knowing your team members well enough to understand their internal development needs and motivational touch points.

The trouble is, even after doing all these things; they may still not act.

We have all witnessed this. We have all struggled with this.

The temptation is to continue to blame ourselves. Have we trained enough? Have we inspired and motivated enough? Are the expectations clear enough? Do they clearly understand the importance of the action?

We may have to come to grips with that; well, many times, we have done all those things. We have often provided the proper tools and training for them to succeed. But even after we've shown someone how to use a hammer and shown them why they should use it to pound in a nail, they still must make the choice to pick it up and give it a swing.

So, where does this leave us? Accountability.

We need to own our actions; they need to own theirs. It is their Action Gap to close...plain and simple. If we honestly look at our past actions and validate that we've provided our team members with the appropriate level of direction and support, they need to be accountable for taking the step. Sure, we need to own creating a culture of action and commitment, but they need to own it.

Repeating training over and over doesn't drive them to take action. They have been trained. They have demonstrated the ability to take action. They've expressed their understanding of... What needs to be done, how it needs to be done, why it needs to be done, and when it needs to be done. More and more training isn't the solution.

There is something deeper than their level of training that is preventing them from taking the action. Talk to them, ask them. Perhaps you'll discover it by building a partnership with them in the quest to uncover the obstacle.

But in the end, we've done our part in leading them to this point; we want them to take the drink of water and take the action. But...it is a choice. The choice is theirs.

27 | LEARNING FROM SUCCESS

Everyone makes mistakes, but mistakes can be good when we learn from them. Right? I mean, that is what our mothers or fathers taught us. "Learn from your mistakes," they'd say. That is how we grow.

I want to point out something else, though. We can also learn from what we do correctly as well. In fact, learning from our wins can be even more powerful than learning from our losses. When we have a winning day or week, if we stop and analyze why we won, we can then repeat it. The miss happens when we celebrate our wins without knowing why or how it happened.

To have something repeated, we need to know how it was done. This is especially true with winning. We are usually pretty good at breaking down our errors or missteps and then correcting the behavior based on that information, but picture how powerful it would be to do the same thing with our wins. Picture breaking down all the steps we took to succeed. What was the language we used? What was our posture like? What execution steps were involved? How did we partner with others?

I always say, "If a report is printed but not analyzed and acted upon, then a tree died in vain." This means that companies, and leaders in particular, are really good at designing reports and even knowing what the data tells them. The breakdown in the process comes when there is no behavior change or reinforcement that happens because of reading the report.

So often, we print a report, see that we've met our goal, celebrate, and then toss the report aside to move on to a new day. When winning happens, we must celebrate. This produces positive momentum! Winning leaders say that we should celebrate for 24 hours and then move on. This is important because it eliminates complacency.

If we are to repeat the success, we must understand why we achieved it. What Performance Gaps were prevented? What talent was involved? What training and teaching did we provide? What expectations were set? What methods of accountability have we used? We mustn't just read the report and set it aside. We must dedicate time to analyze the causes, just as we do when we miss our behavior and result expectations.

By breaking down the win and truly understanding how we achieved it and then repeating the steps we took, we will win again and again.

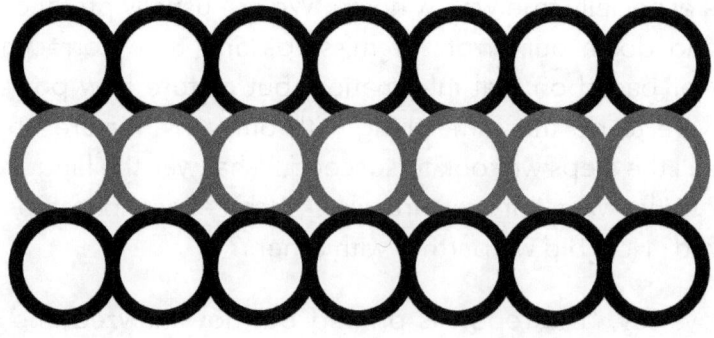

28 | LEGACY

I've been thinking a lot lately about my legacy. It may just be the start of my midlife crisis, but as my boys get older, I feel as though I must leave something behind for them. Not just a physical or financial possession, but instead a memory, a feeling, an inspiration of sorts that they will identify with me as their father. This legacy needs to be something that will stir them into action down the right path in their lives. Every word we speak creates those feelings, and everything I do cements those feelings in their minds for the years to come.

I desire that those memories and feelings are of a passion for life, people, and the world around us. Those memories must reflect the importance of improving things, step-by-step, person-by-person, and situation-by-situation. My boys need to understand that they matter, that the world around them matters, and that how they interact with that world matters.

Their priority list must be clear, and they must focus on themselves first, for without a clear focus on their own internal physical, mental, and emotional health, nothing else they desire will be possible. Next, they need to focus on family. Family is the rock, the foundation from which their support base is built. From there, they need to focus on their work. At this stage of their lives, that work occurs within their schools, but that will change as they age. It is this focus on work that will provide financial stability that will help to minimize stress, and provide amazing world opportunities. Next, they need to focus on the community. Friends and strangers they meet, current and future, will enlighten their lives in fun, exciting, and untold ways and provide opportunities to contribute to society. Finally, all these focuses for them are wrapped in a blanket of personal spirituality that gives them an internal strength of character and integrity.

I desire that the legacy I leave behind for my boys demonstrates this holistic experience of life that creates a better world and inspires them to do the same for themselves and the people they touch as they move through their own years.

In a world of business, do we think about legacy? Gapology embraces many of the things that create a living legacy for the teams we support. Things like creating a Shared Vision, delivering Stump Speeches, and developing clear expectations around Five Focuses align our teams down a path where they will see the "end in mind" and build a method of achieving it.

These visions and inspirational leadership methods close Importance Gaps because they stir the heart and spirit around expectations. They give team members something to believe in and strive for, moving them quickly up the Commitment Ladder from a "compliant" status to a "commitment" level.

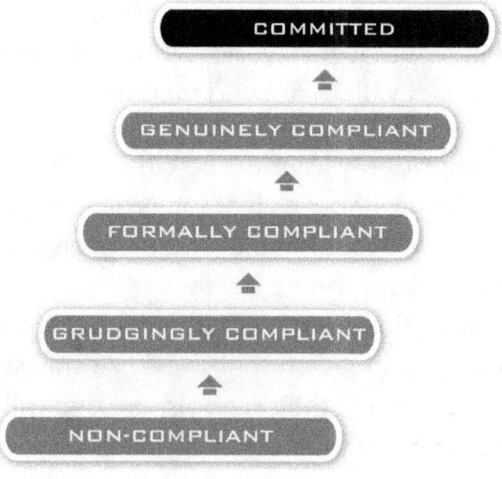

Winning leaders know that they play an essential role in creating this momentum, and they understand that everything they say and, more importantly, everything they do builds their legacy around how they are viewed as a leader within their teams.

Business leaders like Sam Walton, Walt Disney, and Bill Gates have all left tremendous legacies behind them. Their legacies have impacted not only the organizations they left behind but business in general, along with the world around them, and the impact of their leadership will be felt for years and years to come.

We all need to feel the passion for our business, but even more importantly, we must feel the passion for the people that make up the business. It is in the minds of these people that our legacy is built. The things we say and do with them will create action and a spirit of the shared journey we are all on together.

We must inspire them to start with themselves by gaining training and education to improve their talent level. Then, they need to focus on their teammates (their internal family) by helping each other grow in skill by offering challenges, encouragement, and support. Next, they need to focus on the customer, the business, and the work around them to ensure profits are generated that will help the organization continue to grow. They then need to focus on the fun, exciting elements of the business that helps to build camaraderie and lighten the heavy loads being lifted and hauled each day. And finally, all of these must be wrapped around a spirit…a culture…of winning.

In doing these things, not only do we build a culture of winning, but we also leave a legacy of winning!

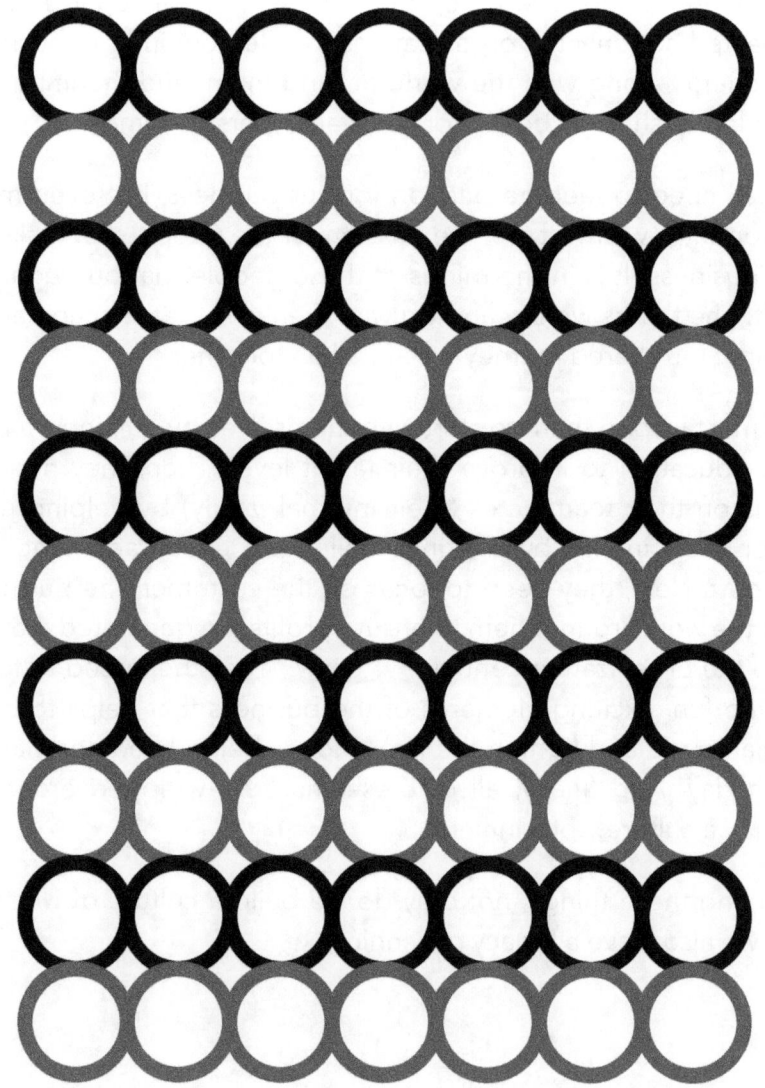

29 | MOTIVATION MYSTERY

What motivates one person and not another? It may be a mystery. But one thing is sure, the Michael Jordans, Nelson Mandelas, Mother Teresas, and Bill Gates of the world were at the top of their fields because of motivation. The specific elements that motivate professional athletes, world leaders, humanitarians, and business leaders are very different. Yet, they are very much the same when it comes to moving them to the point of taking action.

Just think about it. Mother Teresa got out of bed every morning and had one focus in mind, caring for people experiencing poverty in Calcutta. Michael Jordan got out of bed every morning and had one priority: winning basketball games. Two very different focuses…Two very different lives. But they had one thing in common…Motivation.

If we, as business leaders, can tap into that…tap into motivation in the same way as the people mentioned above, we too could make a difference in the world. But what is it? How do we capture it? How do we leverage it in our own lives?

The mystery to unravel is, "What causes motivation?"

World-renowned speaker and life coach Anthony Robbins describes the two things that create motivation as Pain and Pleasure. In his book, Awaken the Giant Within, he says, "The secret of success is learning how to use pain and pleasure instead of having pain and pleasure use you. If you do that, you're in control of your life. If you don't, life controls you."[3]

As a product of nature, we are wired to avoid pain and to seek pleasure. It is in our DNA. It is what drives us.

We may be motivated by money. Not the physical paper itself. After all, the legal pad on my desk does not motivate me, and it is made from the same trees as money. It is the <u>feeling</u> that money provides. It could be the desire for the pleasurable sense of security that money would provide for my family. Maybe it's the pleasurable desire to buy something fun with it. Or…contrast to that, the feeling might be the painful fear that I will suffer if I don't have money. I might lose my home. I might have to live on the street. I might not be able to buy my Starbucks latte.

Weird…the same motivational trigger, money, driven by two different motivational elements.

What drove Mother Teresa? Was it the pleasure she felt when helping people? Was it the pain she feared when she couldn't help people? Money was certainly not a motivator for her, but it was still either the pleasure or the pain she felt that made her devote her entire life to caring for them.

In our world, as leaders, we need to be students…students of the motivational mystery. What makes our team members tick? What type of motivation drives each person who works for you?

---

[3] Anthony Robbins

- Is it pleasure? Do they work hard because they love recognition, bonuses, or customer praise?

- Is it pain? Do they work hard because they would feel awful if they disappointed you or their customers? Perhaps they fear that they might earn less than they need.

Whatever the motivation, it is up to us as leaders to uncover the mystery in each team member. Once we unravel it, we can help provide the right environment for them to be self-motivated to achieve their desires.

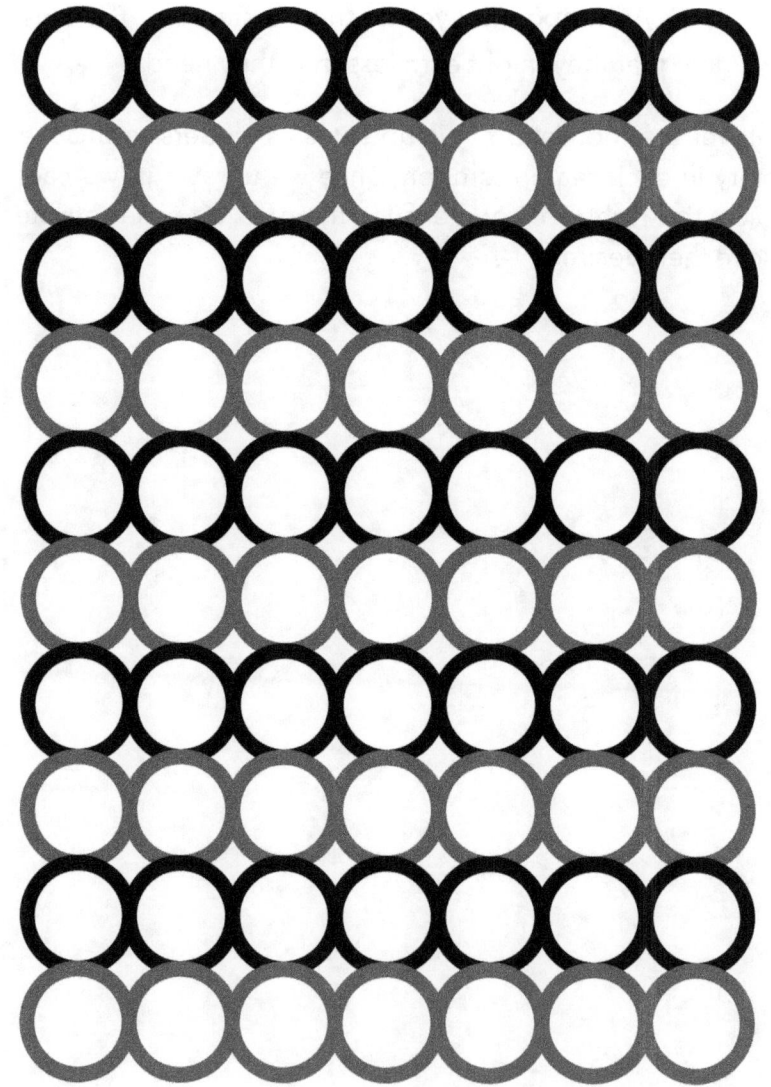

30 | NEW BEGINNINGS

The environment begins to change around the end of May in the United States. We've moved from the long, cold winter through spring and head into summer. It's the season of graduations and weddings. It's the season of new beginnings.

This process of change is a complicated one. When my oldest son graduated from high school, we were excited and proud that he had accomplished such a tremendous milestone in his life. He worked extremely hard for 12 years and deserved the opportunity to stop, reflect, and celebrate his accomplishments.

But once his reflection time was over, reality set in. He would be moving on to college and working and become ultimately responsible for his destiny. He would need to accept the new changes that were ahead of him. The past life is over. He must move past it and on to the new ventures that wait for him. This *transition* can be painful for many people, and it certainly may be hard for him, but the change happens. It is a fact. There is nothing he can do about it. However, we, as parents, need to help him handle the transition.

This process of dealing with the transitions caused by a change in the workplace is a tremendously difficult thing for leaders to help their teams handle as well.

As winning leaders, we must be flexible. Change is something that happens daily in our lives. We will never have long-term success if we can't change and handle the transitions in our business world. This is a fact. Leaders who resist new cultural, procedural, behavioral, or ideological changes will always butt heads with their supervisors and employees. There will always be struggles, conflicts, and high emotions in an environment resistant to change.

We need to remember that, as leaders, we need to be aware of the need to embrace change and be aware of the emotional transition that people will go through during times of change, and finally, understand our role in helping our team members through that transition.

For every ending, there is a new beginning. Between the end and the beginning is the tricky part. This is the phase where the person either makes it or doesn't. This is the phase where winning leaders make their mark on the lives of their team members.

They need to let the past go. They need to understand <u>clearly</u> that the past no longer exists. It cannot be revisited, and the winning leader will ensure this message is clear.

Once they come to grips with the fact that the change is happening, they need to get through the emotional transition. The winning leader needs to understand the emotional sense of loss that everyone goes through during times of high change.

Everyone goes through the DABA Change Model: *Denial* ("This isn't real, it's just a new phase that'll never work."), *Anger* ("Why me? This stinks!"), *Bargaining* (Can we try it this other way instead?"), and *Acceptance* ("How can I help?"). Some people move through DABA quicker than

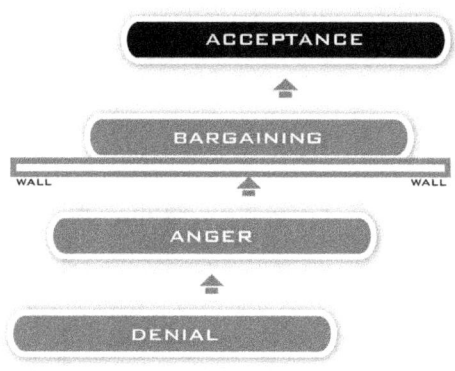

others, and some people get stuck at certain levels, but everyone experiences these phases. It is up to the leader to guide them through it quickly and completely, to the point of Acceptance.

Suppose we have someone who is resisting change. In that case, whether cultural, procedural, behavioral, or ideological, it is up to us as leaders to provide the right amount of direction and support to help them through it. We cannot accept their resistance. Resistance will create Importance Gaps. We must be firm in our resolve and our message, providing the "whys" for the change, providing the benefits of the change, providing the risks for not changing, and providing the clear expectation that they change.

Then, as they are transitioning through the change, we must provide any necessary support for them emotionally to help them finally embrace it.

So... change is not a choice. The <u>decision to transition,</u> however, is up to them, and <u>the decision to lead</u> through the transition is up to us.

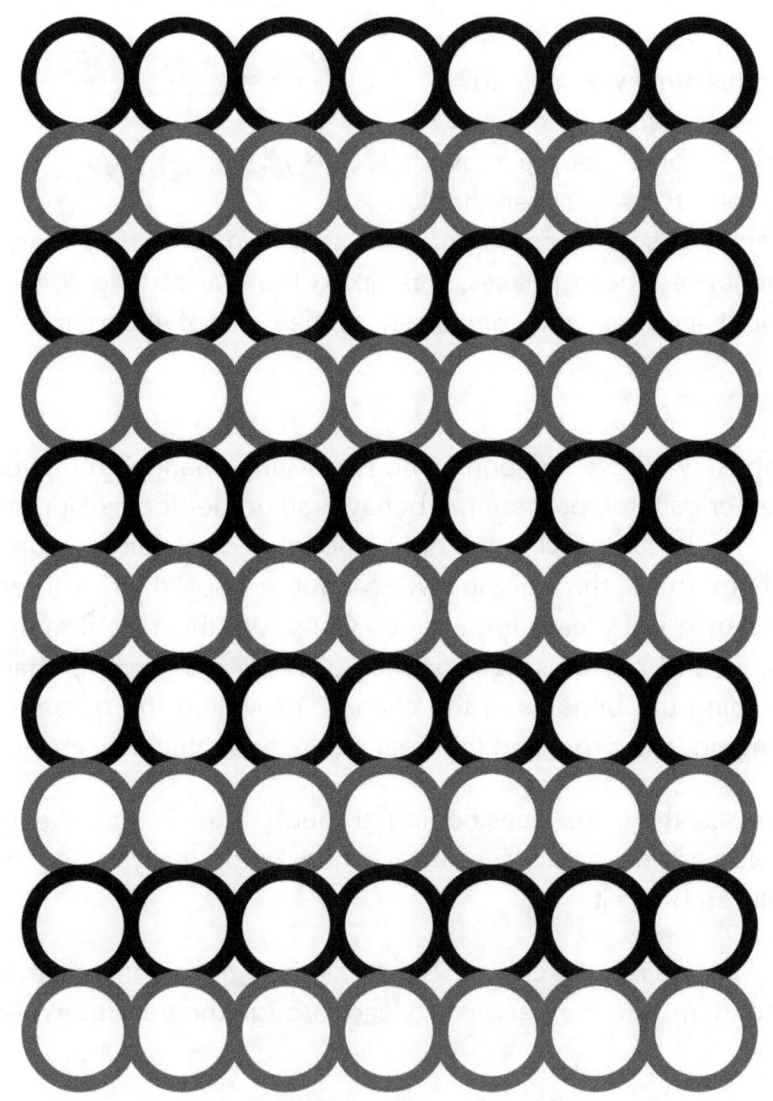

31 | PASSION

Passion...You can't train it...You can't teach it...You CAN inspire it.

What is the difference between "wanna-be" rock stars and real rock stars? Passion. What is the difference between "wanna-be" actors and the real actors? Passion. What is the difference between "wanna-be" leaders and real leaders?... You guessed it...Passion.

Sitting at home on the couch watching an ordinary movie with an ordinary plot and cast does nothing for most people. After two hours, your life is the same; you don't see the world differently...you just wasted two hours. But, every once in a while, a movie like Schindler's List, Terms of Endearment, or Titanic comes around, and the world you're living in changes. Why? After all, it's just a movie.

The difference is the passion inspired by the actors. Liam Neeson, Shirley MacLaine, and Leonardo DiCaprio all played their characters with enormous passion. If they had portrayed them without it, the movies would have been ordinary, but because of the passion in their performances made them extraordinary.

This is also the difference between ordinary leadership and extraordinary leadership. Winning leaders lead with passion. They wake up each morning and intentionally decide to be passionate about their work. They choose to inspire passion in others. They decide to lead.

These decisions to lead with passion drive their desire to move their teams to take action. They ensure their teams know what to do and how to do it. And they do so in a way that inspires the team to want to learn and want to grow in their levels of development.

They ensure that the team understands why things need to be done and when things need to be done. There is no question as to the importance of the actions the team needs to take. Team members understand it and believe in it. They are committed to it. These passionate leaders do not accept less than a team member's total effort. They create accountability around behaviors and results. If a team member doesn't share their passion and refuses to perform, the leader removes them from the team. Only passionate performance can survive in this environment.

Passion is contagious, and it is required in a culture of winning. Passion is inspired, but it is also a choice. We have the ability to decide to live our lives with passion. We can wake up in the morning and live an ordinary day, not inspiring or motivating anyone, and go home at the end of the week and look back at it and think, "What did I do?" Or we can jump up each morning, look out the window, and greet our day with open arms and an open mind to the possibilities ahead. We can look at problems as challenges to overcome. We can look at individual performances as behaviors for us to inspire. We can train, teach, and develop talent. We can set clear expectations, provide clear communication, and determine priorities that lead our teams to take action. We can inspire action.

This is our choice...our decision. Do we live as "wanna-be" leaders? Or live as winning leaders...leaders who live with passion?! Let's choose Passion!

32 | PERSONAL ACCOUNTABILITY

Many are familiar with the story of a young George Washington and his father's favorite cherry tree. Upon discovering his tree was chopped down in his garden, George's father asked his young son who had done it. George replied with a brave voice, *"I cannot tell a lie, Pa. You know I can't tell a lie. I did it with my hatchet."* George's father then did not reprimand him but instead gave him a hug and congratulated his son's heroism in telling the truth.

This story, which many believe to be fictional, was written after our first President's passing by Mason L. Weems, an Anglican pastor and bible salesman. Although possibly a fable, many historians point to the truths behind the story regarding the immense integrity and personal accountability of George Washington and his father, Augustine.

When many leaders consider the word "Accountability," they picture the formal process of holding team members accountable for not performing their duties. They envision counseling sessions built around the process of progressive discipline leading toward terminations.

Winning leaders think of accountability in a much different light. They approach it from the standpoint of creating a culture of personal accountability.

Personal accountability is a seed planted inside team members early in their careers. From their first days with a winning leader, they experience what it is like to win. They feel and understand the importance of their roles and how they contribute to the overall success of their team. They know that they matter. They know that their results matter. They will let their team and leader down if they don't perform at their best every day.

Personal accountability is the emotional driver of motivation and momentum. It pushes team members and leaders to act in a way that is beyond their own needs and wants. It touches their heart and soul, moving their minds and hands to perform to the best of their ability.

There is no room for grudging compliance or non-compliant performance in a culture of personal accountability. Winning leaders quickly remove these performers from their team, and the other team members refuse to allow dissent among their ranks. Only those who actively embrace the culture are

allowed to work and live within it. Because of this culture, the team understands that they are all working together in their joint efforts to create a shared vision around what is important for their team. They move as one. They think as one. They believe as one.

Once this type of culture exists, the winning leader doesn't sit back and enjoy the success. They continue to work hard to maintain it. They know that their efforts create this culture of personal accountability. They continue to train, teach, and coach the talent.

They continue to set clear expectations, communicate, validate, and investigate performance, and establish specific priorities around the behaviors that will drive their result expectations. They build a culture of action by establishing a personal commitment to the greater good of their team and the organization.

The winning leader creates momentum around personal accountability by scorecarding and recognizing top performance publicly and privately in sincere, motivational moments with their team members. They acknowledge those who go above and beyond normal expectations but also give specific thanks for specific behaviors throughout each day.

They know their team and what motivates them and de-motivates them. They support them when they need support and provide direction when they need direction. They work side by side with them and step aside when required. The winning leader understands the fragile balance between leading a team and supporting a team.

George Washington told the truth about the cherry tree, not because he felt that he got caught. He did it because he was personally accountable for his integrity and belief in himself. He could not tell a lie; it was not something he could emotionally do. From a very early age, his father bred this level of accountability in him. Integrity was cultural in his family, and to not live to that high level was unthinkable.

Winning leaders know that they are personally accountable for the success of each and every heart, soul, mind, and set of hands-on their team. They understand and create accountability… not just through the documentation of poor performance but through their yearning to win together as a team. This is true accountability…personal accountability.

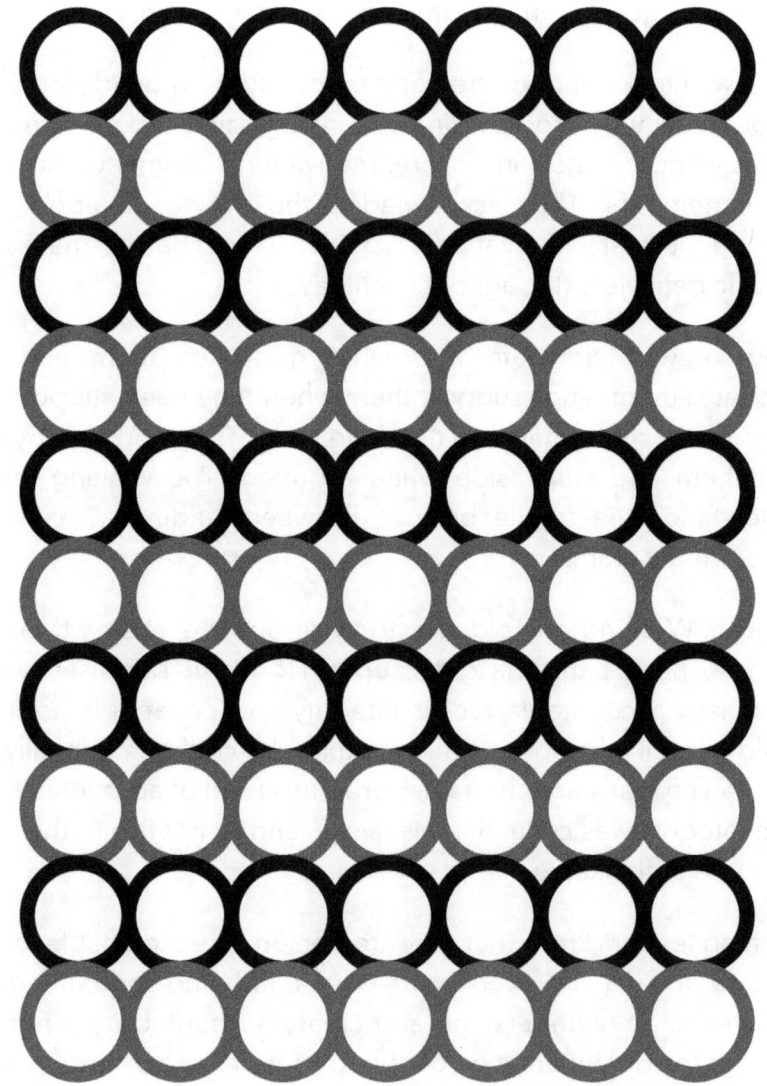

33 | POLISH THE APPLE

A current trend in grocery store retail's highly competitive world is creating truly beautiful produce areas. They stack oranges, pears, and bananas to create displays that are nearly works of art. Many even go so far as to polish the apples to give them a bright shine.

While all apples naturally produce their own wax that protects the fruit's juices from evaporating, commercially washing them removes much of it. Therefore, apple packers must add back wax such as carnauba or other FDA-approved waxes, which protects them once again. This wax gives the apple its shine. And if you polish it, the shine grows.

The same happens with our top talent... our "A" players. They are already beautifully shiny in your eyes and in the eyes of their team members, but if you give them a little polish, their shine will grow, too!

So how do you "polish" them? The easy way is to follow the Gapology order, K-I-A: Knowledge - Importance - Action.

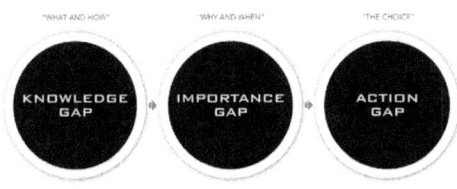 You need to start with their knowledge. Spend extra time with "A" players on your top five focuses. Ask them what part they play in the success of these priorities. How do they impact the results? How do

they impact their team's behaviors? Then validate their knowledge *and skills* by having them demonstrate their role in the priorities. If it is a coaching and support role, observe them coaching a team member. If it is an instructional role, observe them providing instructions. A winning leader validates not just their knowledge but also their skills.

Then continue to their understanding of the importance of the top five focuses. Ask the "A" players why the top five are the top five and how they live them daily. Ask them why it's important for them to execute them. Ask them what your result and behavioral expectations are. Ask them what the priority order is for that specific day. Have them lay out their plan to gain commitment from their team.

Then finish the polish with responsible empowerment. Empower them to tackle new things. Challenge them and push them to raise their own bar. This is where you'll create commitment and gain momentum with them. This is where the apple begins to shine.

Just as there are bad apples in every batch, your team will occasionally pick one up as well. That's understandable; it's natural. A winning leader will quickly identify the bad ones and either help them to cut out the destructive behaviors or they will remove them from the batch.

The key to improving your overall performance is not always to dwell on the bad apples. Winning leadership will eliminate them quickly and efficiently. The key is to spend quality time on the "A" players. Schedule time with them... I should say, "Schedule **quality** time with them." The temptation is to leave them alone to do their job, but many times they get left alone for so long that they start making poor choices on how to perform.

Take care of your "A" players, nurture them, support them, and give them what they need to continue to grow. You don't want them to die on the vine!

So, ask yourself this today, "Who are my shiny apples?" and "How can I help them polish their performance?"

Then... get polishing!

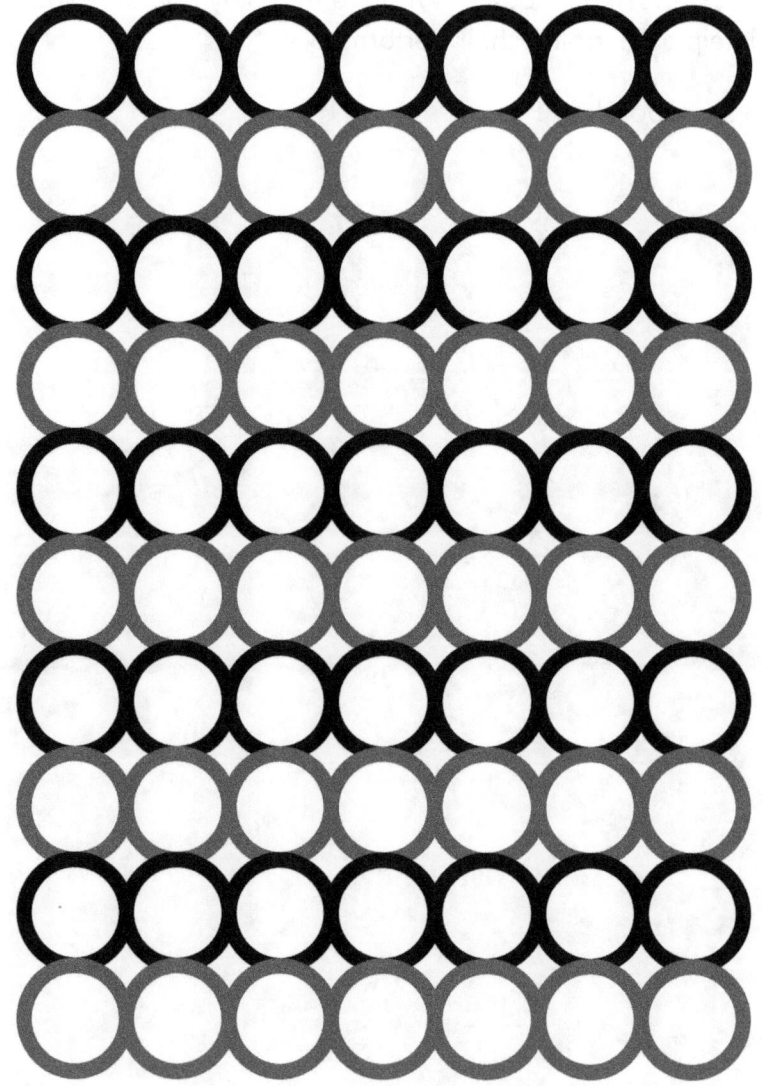

34 | PRISMS

To the average person, a beam of light appears white. However, once the beam hits a prism, that white light bursts into a rainbow of spectral colors. How does this happen?

Sir Isaac Newton discovered that white light isn't actually white. It comprises particles that travel at different speeds, broken out into component colors when slowed down as they pass through the prism.

Winning leaders look at the performance of their team in the same way.

It is easy to look at the overall results and pat ourselves on the back when we win or beat ourselves up when we lose. The Winning leader breaks apart the results and looks at the root causes individually.

We may need to identify the behaviors that created the result by only looking at the result. Sure, it may be considered a "winning result" on the surface because we met our overall goal, but if small individual Performance Gaps were closed, the overall winning results would be much higher. Conversely, we may look at a "losing result" and reprimand the whole team when there are just a few whose poor performance negatively impacts the overall results.

On our teams, many factors contribute to our success or non-success. Like a ray of white light is made up of different particles, so is our team. We have team members who individually work at different speeds and deliver different results. By breaking the team into sections and looking at them as individual contributors, we can quickly identify who is driving the results and dragging them down.

We recommend looking at them in terms of A, B, and C players.

Our "A" players are our top contributing group. These are the ones who are committed to the vision, the plan, and our expectations. These are the ones we should spend the most time with, develop, recognize, and leverage to help the members of the other groups.

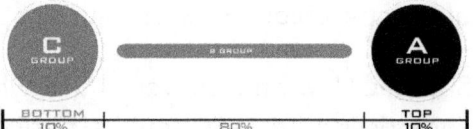

Our "C" players are the ones who are dragging our speed and momentum down. They are grudgingly compliant at best and deliver results that are inconsistent or below our expectations. The winning leader quickly identifies them and moves them to a different group or entirely off their team.

Our "B" player group is the group that truly determines the success or failure of the overall team. This group is typically compliant with the leader's expectations and therefore delivers mediocre results. They are happy being in the middle of the pack because it tends to keep them off the boss' "radar." The winning leader understands this and identifies them. They know that their results will never be consistently great if this group is too large. "B" players must move up to the "A" group if the leader is ever to be considered a winning leader.

Remember, things are not always as they seem. Until Isaac Newton came along, we all thought that light was white. Look at your team through a prism. Who is moving your results and who is dragging down your results, and who is content to be "below your radar?"

Then... take action!

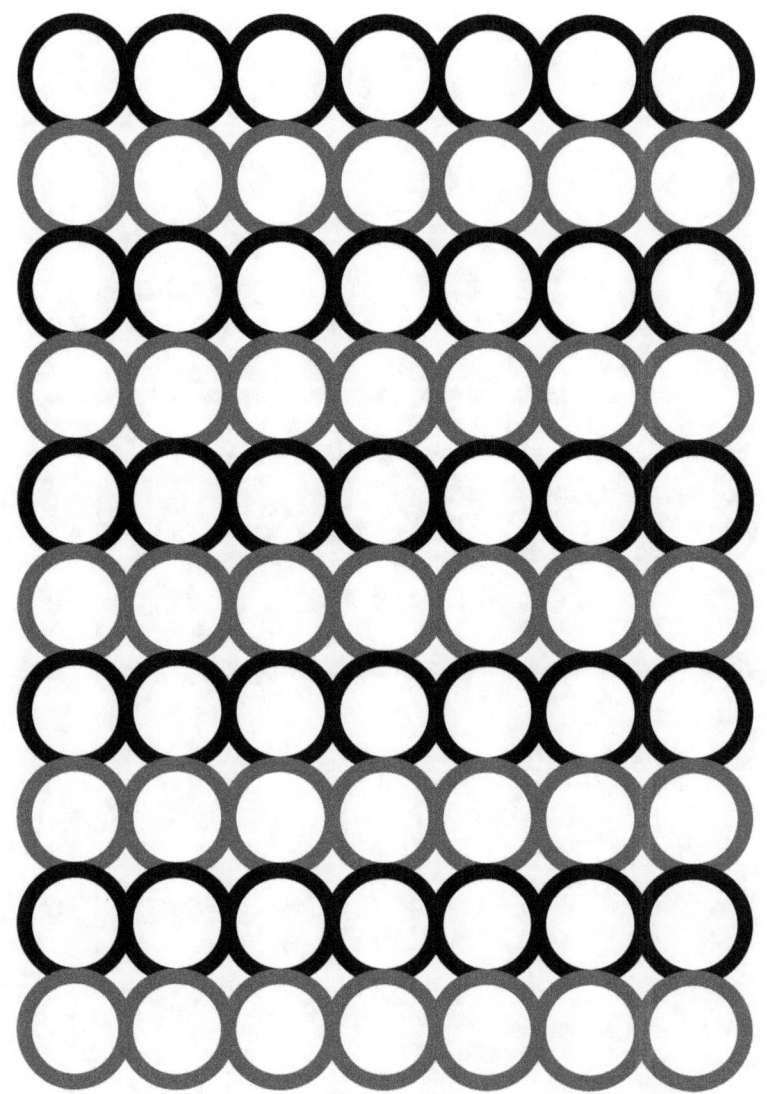

35 | RAISING THE BAR

I was at a wedding recently. This was one of those big, old-fashioned, German Catholic church-type weddings. You know, the kind, the ones where at the reception the buffet lines serve sauerkraut, bratwurst, and potato salad. The type where the grandmothers kiss and squeeze the breath out of everyone, the pre-teens sneak sips of their parents' champagne, and everyone waits impatiently for the conga line to begin so they can do the "chicken dance."

I know you've all been there. You can probably smell the macaroni hot dish right now. (Casserole for you non-Minnesotans)

However, the one thing that always confuses me at these types of events is when someone pulls out the Limbo Stick. For some reason, this crazed person believes that the only way a newly wedded couple will have a long and happy life together is to start their wedding night with a strained neck and a broken back.

The kids, of course, easily run underneath, and the grown-ups suddenly believe that their arthritis, bursitis, or whatever other "itis" type ailment they usually complain about has now been cured by the appearance of this magic pole. Somehow a miracle has just happened, and they're now flexible enough to show off "how low they can go." But of course, all the Limburger cheese and hefeweizen ale they've just devoured gets the best of them, and they end up limping back to their table to discover that their champagne has once again disappeared.

Anyway, this event, particularly the limbo stick, got me thinking. It made me wonder about my own bar. (Not the one in my basement, which I could have been sitting at instead of having grandma crush my ribcage) I'm talking about the "Bar of Performance Excellence," which I set for myself.

Everyone has one of these bars. They may not even realize it, but they have one.

They have set their bar through their individual performance, confidence, competence, commitment, and convictions.

Winning leaders, however, look at where their bar is sitting and make a conscious, intentional decision to continue to raise it. They identify and close Performance Gaps in themselves and their team. They study new things, reach out to peers and supervisors, stretch their comfort zones, and are open to feedback. They don't accept things as being "good enough." They are always strategically reaching for the stars while staying firmly planted on the ground. They look at how their own performance impacts their team and adjust their level of direction and support based on their team members' needs.

In a sense, they continually push the bar higher and higher.

Continuing the Limbo analogy: Is it easier to keep the bar low and constantly struggle to get under it? Or is it easier, in the long run, to take the necessary steps to set our sights higher and move the bar?

Sure...moving our bar takes some work. We may struggle to lift and then hold the bar higher. Our arms may shake and become weary. But...all the strain will make us stronger, and as we build our muscles, it will become easier to hold the bar. Then, the act of walking underneath will be a breeze.

This week, take a look at your own "Bar of Performance Excellence" and determine what <u>new</u> steps you can take to raise it. Your back will thank you.

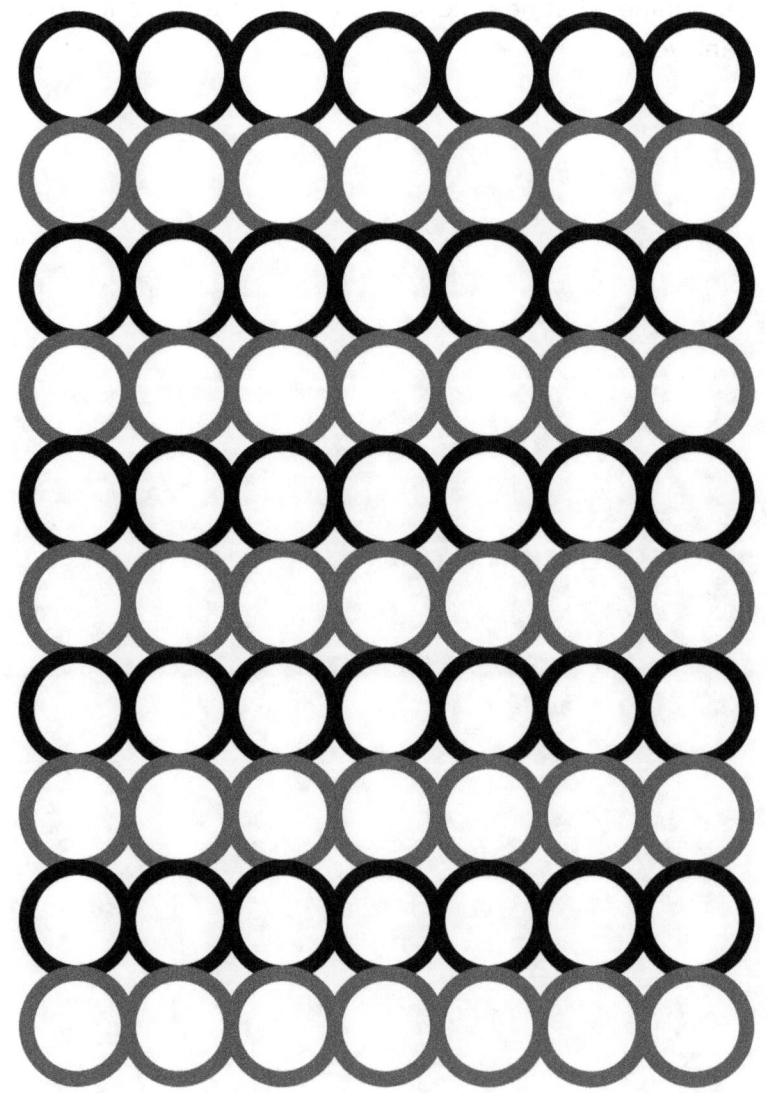

36 | ROLLER COASTERS

Most people love roller coasters...not me exactly...but many others do.

It's hard to say why I don't like them. Maybe it's my *acrophobia* (fear of heights) that gets me. Or perhaps it's a combination of my *basophobia* (fear of falling), *claustrophobia* (fear of confined spaces), *tachophobia* (fear of speed), or *emetophobia* (fear of vomiting). Maybe it's just simply my *thanatophobia* (fear of death).

Roller coasters, in one form or another, have been around since the 1700s and have excited thrill-seekers ever since. They thrill because they take their riders to unbelievable heights and then plummet down to what seems like the edge of disaster and then back again.

While roller coasters are a fun way to spend a day with family or friends, we'd better watch out for them in the business world! Roller coaster performances can really damage an organization's and a leader's credibility, relevance, results, and team.

When looking at your results, you should know that you have tremendous Performance Gaps if you notice a roller coaster effect (exceeding expectations one day and then not meeting them the next). These indicate that Gaps you previously may have thought were closed remain open.

I have witnessed this a million times. Often, following a training workshop, we see a nice bump in our results. We know the movement and begin to pat ourselves on the back, glowing in the knowledge that we made a difference in the lives of our team.

Then, just as swiftly, the next week, we see the results slip back to the previous levels. We provided top-notch materials, activities, and facilitators. We've done all we could to ensure that we set up our learners for success. And then, they perform for a short period and then fall backward to old behaviors.

Why? Did we do something wrong?

Well, many times, the answer is yes. We are tempted by the thought that "telling is training." This isn't true. *"Telling ain't Training!"*

We must ensure that we provide opportunities for our team members to visualize the process through demonstrations or videos, then discuss the new behaviors, ask questions and receive answers and finally get their hands on it and work through the process themselves while receiving coaching from us. And finally, they must be allowed to practice it fully until they can repetitively demonstrate to us that they have the skills to perform to our level of expectations.

After we do this, they must understand the new behavior's importance and where it sits on their priority list. The leader has a tremendous job to fill here. This area is where many teams hit the bottom part of the roller coaster. They don't understand *why or when* they should be doing the new thing. They forget to do it because it isn't a habit or think other things are more important. Or worse yet, they make a conscious choice not to do it!

Winning leaders need to help their teams through this stage. We cannot assume that it will get done just because we have told them to do something and have shown them how, why, and when it needs to be done. This roller coaster of results performance indicates that the Importance Gap is not closed for them. If the leader doesn't communicate properly with the team members and help them set their priority list, they will set it for themselves. Of course, that list will most likely not be in the same order as you would set it.

So, enjoy the roller coaster at the amusement park. Look for ways to close the Importance Gap and level out the peaks and valleys to raise your team's overall performance to new heights!

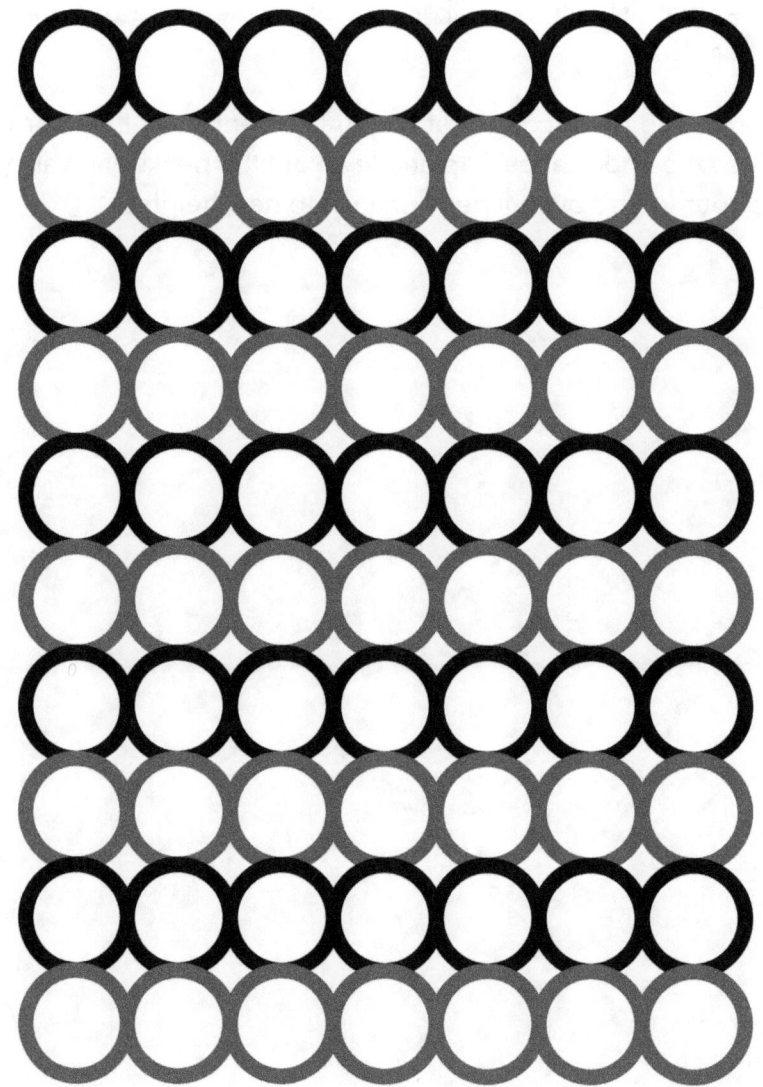

37 | ROOKIES

Everyone, even a Winning leader, begins his or her career as a rookie. We work hard, get recognized, and then get promoted to our first role as a leader of others. This new role comes filled with challenge, excitement, and a little fear.

We knew what to do in our previous role. As individual contributors, we just had to work hard. We did things. We got things done. We were filled with confidence in our abilities. We were in complete control of our destiny.

But things have changed in our new role of being a leader of others. We are now responsible for everyone else. Their performance determines our performance. We must now control things without the use of our own two hands. We now need to step out of the tactical world of doing things and move into the new world of leading others to do things. This is frightening...at least it can be if we haven't been set up for success.

This is where many companies create Performance Gaps, especially Knowledge Gaps. The new leaders are put in their new roles and shown how to do all the new tactical processes and procedures, but true leadership skills are undeveloped. Things like conflict resolution, coaching, counseling, time management, and team recognition are left for the rookie to discover on their own. They end up learning through "trial and error," in the meantime, their frustration levels grow to the point where a once highly confident and committed team member feels defeated. It is at this point where many of them struggle and may even eventually decide to move on to a new position somewhere else. These feelings of inadequacy, fear, and frustration are considerable contributors to turnover in all organizations.

These rookies can be saved, however. Given the environment described above, becoming a second-season team member is quite an accomplishment. We can help them get there. We can create a Teaching Organization where our rookies thrive and grow into long-term veterans. We must determine the right steps and commit to taking them with our teams.

First, and most importantly, we need to train them. We need to train them on the tactical pieces, but we cannot forget to train them on the leadership pieces as well. We need to understand where those frustration points happen with our rookies, and then we must eliminate them.

We need to role-play situations where they are in tough conversations with our customers. Often, they will see a young leader and take advantage of or challenge them. Our rookies must know how to handle these events smoothly and confidently.

We also need to role-play examples of leading other team members. Often, these rookies are younger...much younger... than the veterans they must now lead. We must address the new skills they need to succeed in these challenging relationships. Do they know how to talk to the older vets? Do they know how to resolve issues with them? Do they know how to hold them accountable for behaviors or results? Do they know how to coach them? Do they know how to motivate and recognize them? If we haven't practiced these skills with the new leaders, chances are they don't know how to do these things. Also, chances are that these areas create high levels of stress, anxiety, and frustration for them.

Do the rookies know how to lead younger team members? The younger ones may see the new leader as a peer than a manager. They may push back and challenge them as well. They may try to pull something with them just to see how they react. We need to set them up for success with this group, too.

We must role-play all these scenarios with the new managers so they have positive experiences from which to draw quality leadership behaviors. If we don't, they will just have to improvise what they think is right. In this improvisation, many of them fail, and these failures create poor customer and associate experiences and overall poor results. The improvisations create Gaps that prevent the team from reaching its objectives and expectations.

The beauty in knowing this is that we can now make adjustments. We can ensure that this front-line manager or supervisor gets the knowledge and skills to do their job. We can close the Knowledge Gap permanently for them. With this Gap solidly closed, our new rookies will be set up for success. Their competence will be higher, their confidence will be higher, and their commitment will be higher. With these new and improved levels, our team will be stronger and more ready to meet any challenge thrown its way. Whether we have our seasoned, veteran leaders at the helm or our rookies, our results will be the same. Winning!

38 | SAILING AND SNORKELING

For anyone who's taken a trip to someplace warm and exotic, you may have run into these phenomena.

Some people like to sail, and some people like to snorkel.

Now, I know that both are fun activities, and they are both done in the water, but the elements around them are very different.

Unless you are the captain and you're steering the boat, sailing involves sitting down, skimming along the water's surface, and relaxing with your favorite choice of beverage. The wind and the sails do the work. You just zip along quickly and have a great time enjoying the sunshine. But... you're not really seeing what lies beneath the surface. You hang on and enjoy the ride.

Snorkeling involves work. First, you need to receive some training, put on a life vest, make sure you have the right mask and snorkel, and then you must jump into the water and make an effort to swim around. Also, jumping in, for some, can be frightening because they don't know what is in the water, or they fear getting water in their mask or down their snorkel.

But...the work and the fear are worth the rewards.

The beauty that lies beneath the surface is amazing. The unbelievable wildlife is something you will always remember. The fish, the plants, and the experience of being up close and personal with them can be life-changing.

These two choices are very similar to the choices we, as leaders, must make when leading a team of people.

The first choice is like the sailing example. You can just sit back and enjoy the ride. You don't take an active role in the world around you. You let the team sail along without getting involved with them or their work. This choice is easy.

The second choice is much harder. It takes a winning leader who prepares themselves with the right training and tools and then jumps right in. This leader understands that what they are going to do may be a bit frightening as they might run into Performance Gaps along the way. Problems, obstacles, and challenges may jump out to scare them and derail their focus and efforts.

Jumping in takes effort to be successful. You must take an active role in the world around you. You must get up close and personal with your team members and learn what they need to be successful. You must let them know that you care and appreciate their efforts. You have to show that you're interested in their interests. You must ask questions, and offer advice and support. You must communicate with them.

Jumping in is what builds morale and the overall culture that builds a team. Overcoming the initial fear of jumping in will reward you many, many times over.

Of course, the ones who sail along, relying on the wind to carry them forward, will enjoy themselves, but those who take the risk and take the challenge of jumping in will experience far greater rewards.

39 | SKILL BUILDER

Skills…The final frontier…Well, ok…it's not *Star Trek*… and it's not science fiction.

However, building skills to close Knowledge Gaps is the ultimate destination for anyone conducting training. Many times, we get lost in the information. We focus on delivering our material, making sure that we are heard, making sure that we avoid the "um's and ah's" in our speeches, and making sure that we don't sweat too much during our deliveries. Many times, the one thing we forget is the learner.

The learner is the most important person in any classroom, conference hall, or during those face-to-face teaching sessions. As hard as it is for many of us to believe, it's not about us. It is about the learner. After all, our primary role as leaders is to develop our team members to create strong, self-sufficient, and effective performers.

Of course, any good teaching event begins with quality material that is easy to understand and easy to put into practice. But even the material must be designed with the learner in mind. The crucial thing is to understand where it is that we want the learner to end up…what skill we are trying to build. Once we grasp that result expectation level, we can work backward to create material that will effectively complete this task.

Then, the rubber meets the road for the winning leader.

Adults have specific needs when they learn. They are very different from children.

Here are the four key adult learning principles we need to remember:

1. Adults learn when they feel the need to learn, and the content is relevant to them personally.

2. Adults learn best when their unique experiences are considered.

3. Adults learn best and retain more when a variety of instructional approaches and contexts are used.

4. Adults need practice and feedback until they are successful in a behavior.

Adults learn through a process of discovery and practice. They have a need for a blended teaching approach that folds all learning types into the curriculum.

- They must be shown the steps and how they apply to their current roles. They need to see the end result if they follow those steps. (SHOW)

- They must discuss the process, ask questions, get emotionally involved, and determine how their current base of knowledge applies to these new things. (TELL)

- They need to dive in and get their hands dirty by doing the steps themselves, all while receiving coaching and recognition for their performance. (DO)

- They need to practice the steps over and over until they become a winning performer who meets your level of behavioral and results expectations on a consistent basis. (PRACTICE)

Knowing and embracing the adult learning principles and following the blended teaching approach will make your training stand out and deliver the results we desire as winning leaders.

We must move our learners up the Habit Ladder. We need to start with building Knowledge by ensuring that they have received solid *Communication* of the specific learning material, have complete *Understanding* of the required steps involved, and *Agreement* around those steps. Then we must build their skills through a series of *Practice* sessions that are repeated with coaching over and over to the point where they have built a *Habit Behavior*.

Only with this Habit Behavior the learner will live long and PROSPER!

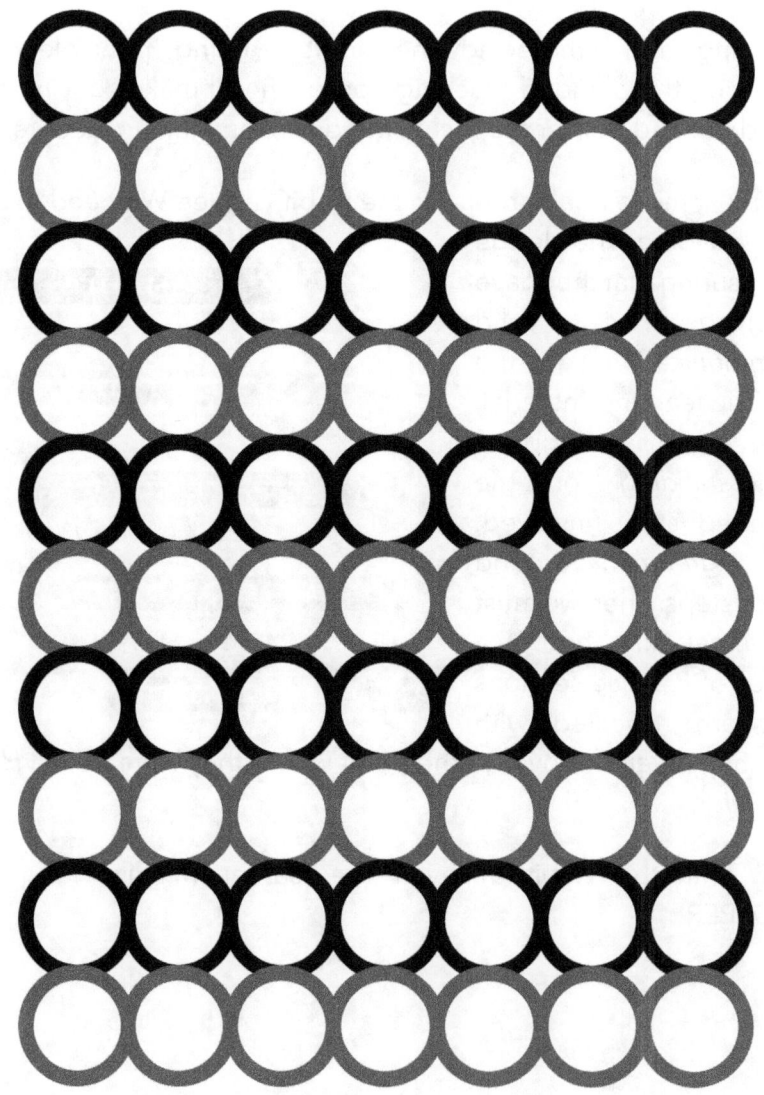

40 | SMELL THE SMOKE

"Where there's smoke...there's fire."

I'm sure that most of you have heard this quote in the past. As leaders, part of our responsibilities is to handle the different fires that start in our work lives. These fires could be big (i.e., a robbery, harassment accusation, a lost contract) or small (i.e., a customer wants to cancel an order, a retail display is set wrong, or the restaurant windows need cleaning). Either way, it is important that the fire gets put out.

A small fire, like a match, is easy to put out. Perhaps it takes one step to handle it. We can just walk over to the match and snuff it out. Easy as that!

The danger, however, is when that small match isn't put out. What happens, then? Well, the small match then starts another fire that then grows and grows and grows until it becomes a blazing bonfire. The simple act of blowing out the match has now become the bigger act of calling 911.

Of course, the big bonfires require immediate action as well. This might mean digging out the fire extinguisher immediately to ensure the blaze doesn't consume our lives and us.

Let's apply this to our business.

If a team member gently mentions that he or she felt uncomfortable with a statement made by a coworker, this could be a match today and easy to handle. However, if left to smolder, this coworker could really set the store "on fire" with inappropriate comments and actions, resulting in formal complaints or even lawsuits.

Quick, decisive action could really prevent these types of firestorms from happening! Winning leaders use E.D.G.E. They exhibit high Energy and are Decisive. They aspire for Greatness and set Expectations around the things that will drive the results they desire. They quickly locate the fires and put them out.

How do they do it? After all, potential fires happen daily.

They start with "Smelling the Smoke." They know that if something smells like smoke, a fire is probably burning.

If they smell the smoke, they:

- Ask questions

- Take a partner in decision-making if necessary

- Take action

Not taking action will not stop a fire. Not taking action allows it to grow.

Of course, the best way to stop a fire is to prevent one, just like ensuring that the pile of kindling isn't sitting next to the fireplace while it's burning. Benjamin Franklin said, "An ounce of prevention is worth a pound of cure."

Make sure that Performance Gaps are closed, policies are followed, expectations are clear, and standards are high. These things will help to prevent fires from starting, and then taking quick action on the ones that do will keep our businesses from burning to the ground.

Smell the Smoke!

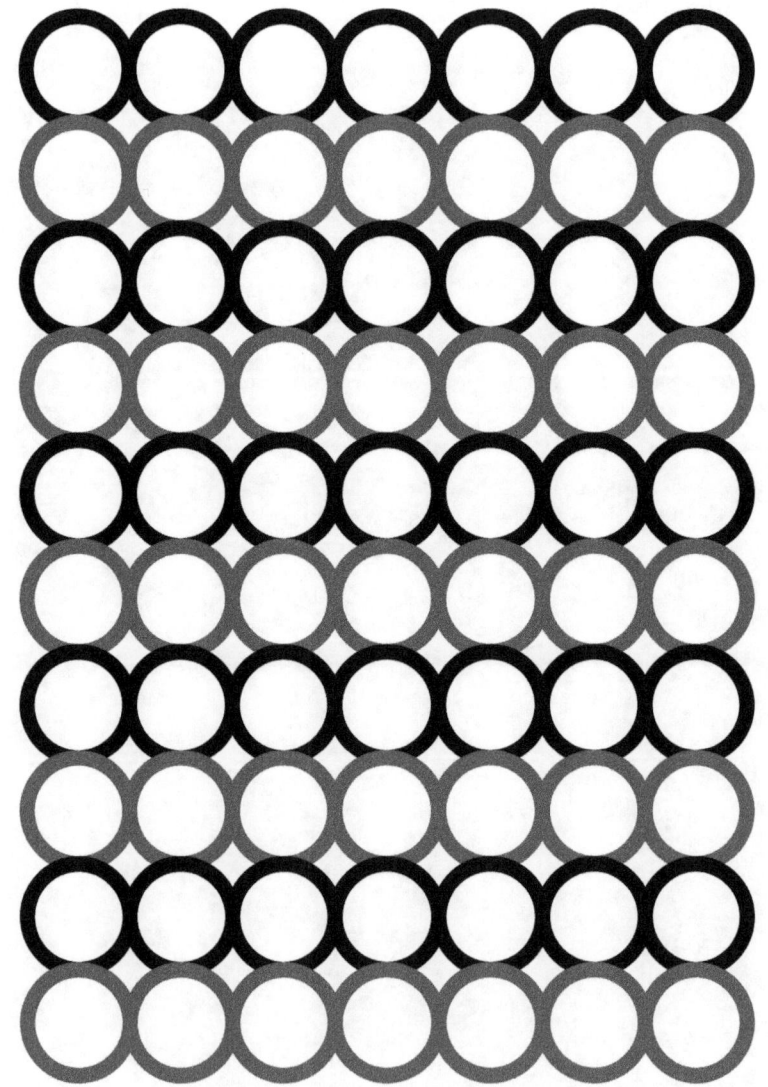

41 | SOCRATES, PLATO, AND ARISTOTLE

Greece in the Middle Ages was the place to be if you loved deep thinking, and three historical figures stood at its center: Socrates, Plato, and Aristotle.

Socrates was a great philosopher who lived around 469-399 B.C. and taught in and around Athens. He is credited as a founder of Western Philosophy and was especially recognized for his contributions to the study of ethics.

Plato was a student of Socrates. He was such a strong believer in Socrates' teachings that he took what Socrates taught verbally and wrote it down in a series known as the Socratic Dialogue, a collection of moral and philosophical teachings. Plato was also known for his teachings on philosophy and mathematics and founded the first institute of higher learning in the Western world, The Academy in Athens.

Aristotle was a student of Plato. His writings were the first to create a comprehensive Western Philosophy system encompassing morality, logic and science, politics, and metaphysics. His teachings carried through until Isaac Newton made his 17th-century discoveries in physics. Many of his teachings exist today and are currently taught in colleges and universities worldwide.

So, if you like to think deeply about philosophy, science, mathematics, and metaphysics, you are probably very aware of these three's tremendous impact on the world. If not, and you are just an average person like me, there is one major piece of teaching you can learn from these men...

To become a great teacher, you must first become a great student.

To create a Teaching Organization, winning leaders begin by opening their minds to both the big picture and the details. They look for the reasons behind things, the cause and effect of the actions taken or not taken. They ask questions of their team members and strive to discover what results were caused by what behaviors.

Winning leaders don't just let things happen by chance. They are strategic in using Gapology in everything they do. They determine and communicate results and behavioral expectations. They develop skills and knowledge. They inspire a feeling of importance and commitment. They measure results and take action based on them, creating a culture of celebration and accountability.

Winning leaders seek out information. They determine why things occur and whether the behaviors can or should be repeated. They are students of behaviors and results.

Then they teach. They take their team members under their wings and create a feeling of safe learning, pushing them to stretch themselves to build new skills. They train completely in the tactics that must be followed to achieve success. They teach the emotional drivers that tap into the learner's spirit. They are only satisfied when they've developed wisdom in the new winning leaders.

One thing I left out of the story of the ancient philosophers...the learning continued. Aristotle became the tutor of Alexander the

Great, who created and led one of the largest empires in ancient history.

Students become teachers. Winning students become winning teachers...and winning leaders. Begin your education today.

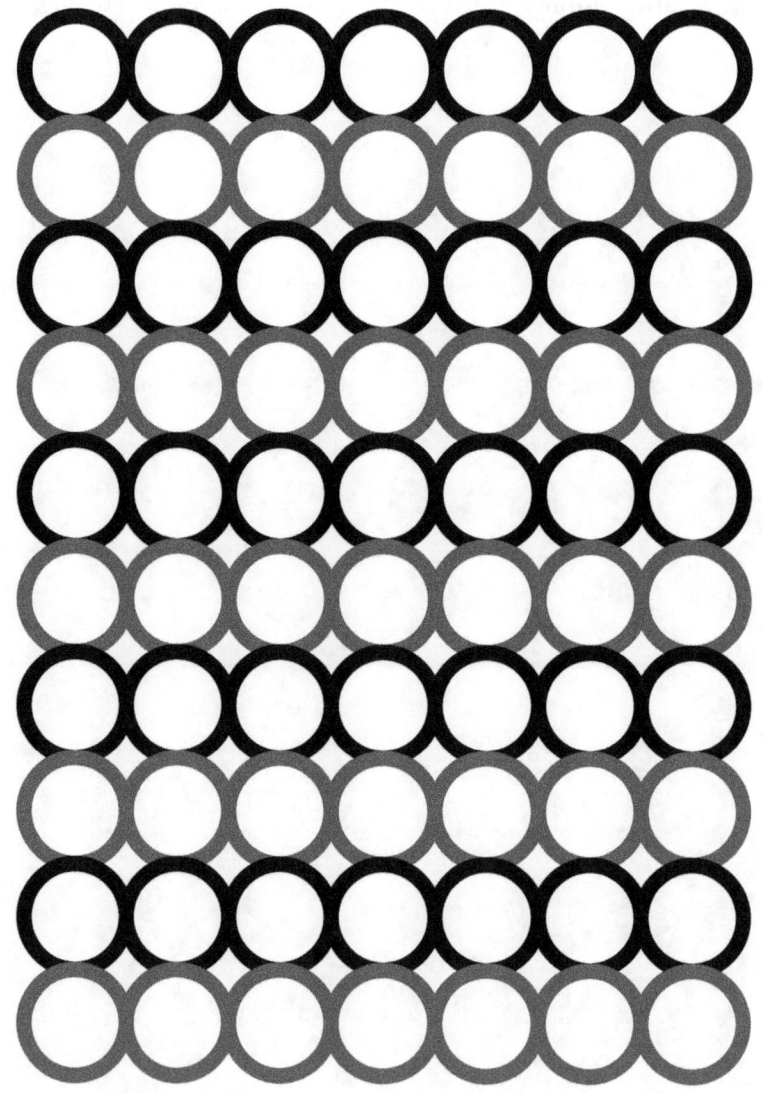

42 | STAKE IN THE HEART

With all the fervor around vampire movies and books lately, there is an interesting element that I'd like to explore. That is the "Stake in the Heart" method of killing vampires.

The word "vampire" has been around since 1734, and the mythological stories of the undead started with John Polidori's book, *Vampyre,* in 1819 and grew exponentially with Bram Stoker's, "Dracula" in 1897. Now, we have the popular *Twilight* series and the HBO show *True Blood*. While the current versions vary quite a bit from the original folkloric tales of vampires, one consistent method throughout history that had been stopping them was a stake through the heart.

Why did authors and movie creators decide to use a stake? And why does it have to be stabbed in the heart?

The reasons for the stake aren't entirely clear, but the obvious relationship is that where the heart goes, so does the spirit, and so does the body.

So, knowing this, as leaders, how do we leverage this concept of "where the heart goes, so does the spirit and the body" with our teams?

We need to tap into their heart. We need to understand where their core beliefs, motivations, and levels of commitment come from.

Once we can understand who they are, what they believe, and what they are passionate about, we can create a partnership with them to help them achieve their goals.

They need to have a different type of "stake." They need to have a stake in the game. If they feel a personal connection to the objectives and expectations of their leader and the organization, their heart will follow. Their personal rewards will be dependent upon their performance in meeting the objectives. Once they understand this, they will work harder to ensure they win.

Just like the towns and villages in the 1800s that gathered with torches and pitchforks to fight a common threat, our teams will gather with the same passion to fight a common fight. If we can tap into a similar, although more reasonable, team mentality that mobs have, our team members will also carry torches for us.

So how do we tap into that mentality? How do we discover the contents of our team members' hearts?

We need to talk to them. We need to listen to them. We must show that we care about them, their passions, and their personal success. *Communication* is a key Root Solution for identifying and closing the Importance Gap, and with strong, proactive communication, many Importance Gaps can be <u>prevented</u> in the first place.

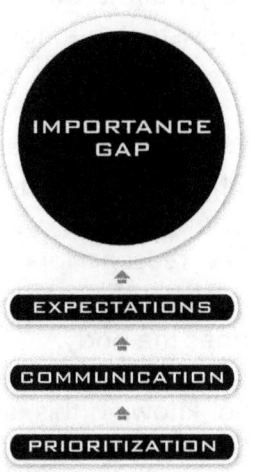

Once we do this, we'll build the relationship, learn about their spirit, and gain their commitment, leading to closing and preventing Action Gaps. We'll gather them together for a common goal and a common purpose.

In fiction, once we understand the desires of a vampire, its patterns, and its methods, we are better equipped to eliminate them. In the real world, once we understand the desires of our team members, their passions, and their motivators, we are better equipped to lead them to achieve common goals and meet our expectations.

While you might not want to talk to a vampire, you do want to talk to your team to determine if they have a "stake" in the game and the "heart" to win.

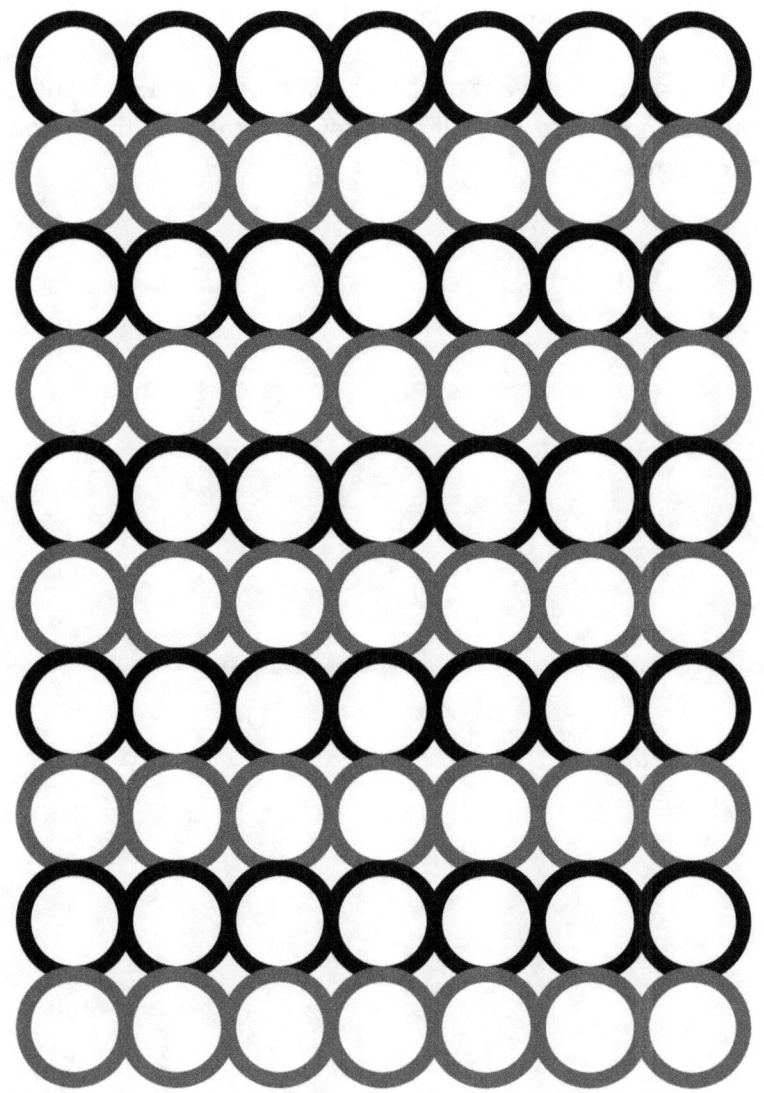

43 | SWEAT THE SMALL THINGS

"Don't sweat the small stuff, and it's all small stuff." That's what they say.

What I'd like to add to this thought process given to us by Dr. Richard Carlson in his famous book series by the same name is...Small things can make a big difference![4] In business, occasionally, what we might consider small things are really big things in disguise!

Just think of the impact of:

- One 5-minute coaching conversation each week with one of your team members. That would total out to be 260 minutes or 32.5 workdays worth of dedicated, strength-building, one-on-one time with that person. How much stronger would he or she be at the end of that year?

- One hour of reading professional-development books each day would amount to 45 workdays of professional development dedicated to building your own skill level.

Wouldn't these results be fantastic? Spending such a small amount of time on developing yourself and developing your team

---

[4] PH.D., Richard Carlson. Don't Sweat the Small Stuff...And It's All Small Stuff. Hyperion, 1996.

members, once you apply the power of time to the equation, makes a tremendous difference.

Stacking small things together doesn't just increase performance in a linear manner. Many times, the small things create exponential improvement as well.

Consider this:

The one-hour reading session is focused on coaching. Your proficiency in coaching is now improved, so your one 5-minute session with your team member delivers a much stronger result. In fact, the coaching improved your team member's talent level so much that you now look to that person to help mentor and train other team members. He then does so well that he gets promoted, and the team members he trained have improved their performance level so much that one of them gets promoted to fill his spot! Exponential growth creates overall momentum within the team.

Of course, Dr. Carlson is certainly correct to state that we mustn't blow things out of proportion. We must see things as they are and not lose touch with the "magic and beauty of life." In business, we must also understand that "Small things can make a big difference." Spend time on the small things, and you will see big results...and possibly sweat a whole lot less!

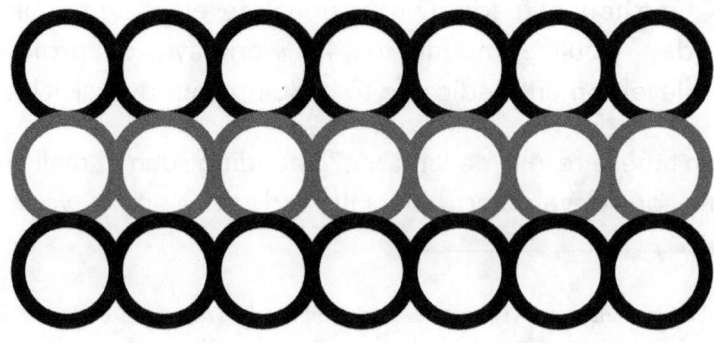

44 | THE ENDING

I've never run a marathon, clearly evident if you've ever met me, but in sitting on my couch eating nachos and watching the runners toil mile after endless mile, I've discovered something. They seem to have such drive, determination, flexibility, and focus.

They've set a result expectation to cross the finish line in a predetermined time frame and a behavioral expectation for themselves to not give up. They keep striving, battling their competition, the clock, and themselves. Then, after 26.22 miles, they cross the finish line.

This is where the amazing thing happens. Many collapse in complete exhaustion. Paramedics carry some away. Several just throw their arms up in celebration, walk off the pain, and go home. But for everyone, the first thing they do is check their time. They want to know how they did. Was the pain worth it? Did they beat their best previous time? Where did they rank in the group? These are the first questions that go through their minds.

Now the best runners don't just end with this bit of information. They don't think, "Well, yeah...I made it in less than 4 hours. Great. Now, where's the Burger King?" Instead, they take the information and start to break it down.

They ask themselves, "Where did I lag a bit in the race? Should I have eaten more carbs the night before? Should I have pushed the first leg of the race a bit harder? What can I do better next time?" The race doesn't stop for them at the finish line. **The finish line is just the beginning of the next race.**

For winning leaders, the same thing holds true.

When many leaders meet a specific result expectation, they stop and celebrate, and then they just move on, driven by the momentum of meeting the result. Certainly, celebrating wins is an important step to build momentum with the team. They need to feel a strong sense of pride in their efforts, so congratulations are definitely appropriate.

Winning leaders, however, take it a few steps further. They stop and celebrate, of course, but they also dissect their win. They stop and reflect, looking at their own "stopwatch" to measure their results. They need to understand exactly how they achieved that win.

They break everything down. "What specific leader behaviors moved the team? What specific team behaviors produced which specific result? What efforts could have been even stronger and allowed us to perform even higher? What Knowledge Gaps were there in my team and in me? What Importance Gaps were there? What Action Gaps were there?" They look for evidence to support the exact outcome that was produced. And then they take action.

Winning leaders apply the information they've identified and begin closing Gaps immediately. They don't wait for the dust to settle on the win before they begin taking new actions to improve their results to an even higher level. They understand that to build true momentum, analysis and action must be a continuous process, and the right action will continually produce the right results.

Winning leaders understand that the ending is never truly the ending…it's just the new beginning.

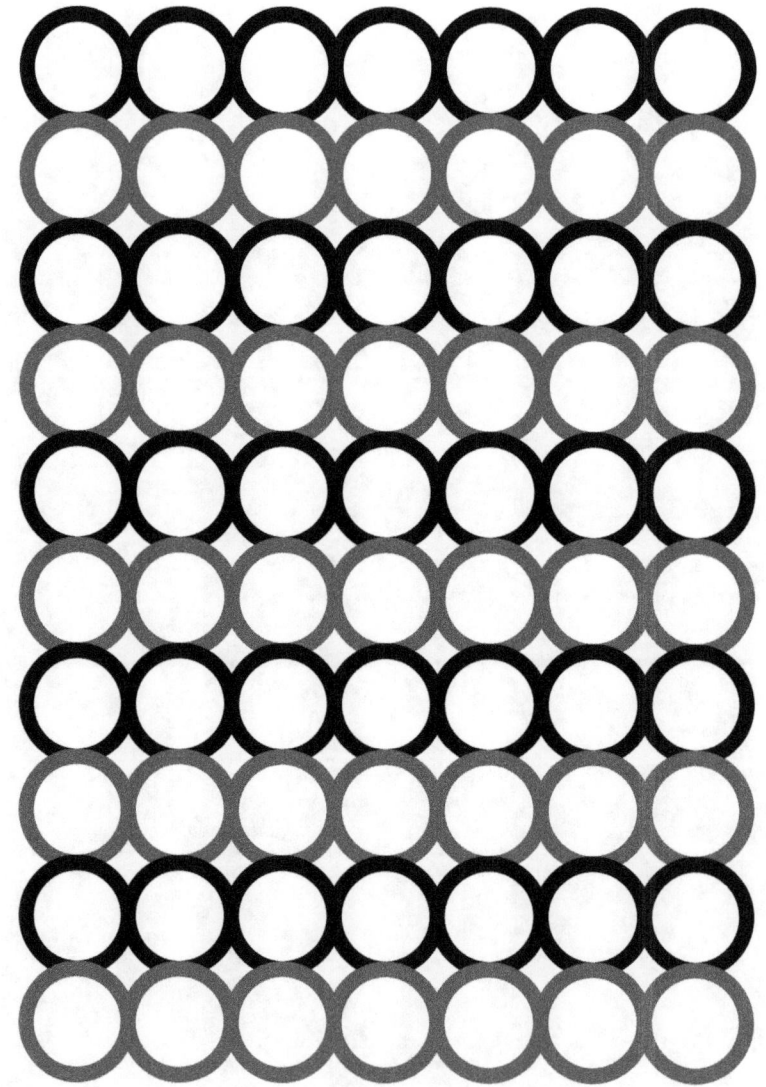

45 | THE ONE THING

I'm often asked, "What is the one thing that is most important for a leader to do daily?" My answer is this…Coaching. Plain and simple.

If a leader is good at coaching, anything is possible. Training is easier, teaching is easier, hiring and developing talent is easier, setting clear expectations is easier, communication is easier, prioritizing is easier, accountability is easier, and celebration is easier. All these Root Solutions to close Performance Gaps are easier and made possible through effective coaching.

Picture the perfect world. As a winning leader, you come in to work worry-free each day. You arrive, walk in, and your business hums like a well-oiled machine. The customers are getting helped. The tactical elements are getting handled. Little problems are solved before they become big problems. Customers rush to your door because they know that they will have a great experience...and they do.

Your sales grow. Your profit grows. Your associate satisfaction grows, and because your team members are happier, they give better customer service, and then sales continue to grow. Your business is in a virtuous cycle that is rolling with momentum.

How did all of this come to be? ... You coached.

You stopped the whirlwind of activities and took an intentional, conscious look at your team. You verified where each team member was in their level of skills and knowledge. You determined what made them tick. You learned what they were motivated by and how they best learned. You leveraged that information to create the perfect training plan for them. You then facilitated the training using multiple styles and kept in mind how adults learn. You asked them for their ideas and input on what they need to be successful. You then gave it to them in a variety of ways. You provided your perceptions on what you saw as opportunities and strength areas. You then helped them to move past any obstacles that stood in their way. You then provided continued support and follow-up to ensure that they performed to your level of expectations consistently and that the behaviors became a habit for them.

Leaders must move their teams to action. They must determine the exact behavior that will create winning results and then train, develop, and create importance around those behaviors and results. Many leaders do this part, but winning leaders also coach. They determine current levels of performance. They identify Gaps in performance. And then they close those Gaps through coaching.

The purpose of coaching, contrary to many current definitions, is to improve performance. Its purpose is not disciplinary action. Coaching is done to move team members to greater performance and help them win bigger.

By improving performance through coaching, fewer "write-ups" need to happen, and a culture of development and winning is created. Teams begin to expect development and growth. They seek it out. They begin teaching others themselves and accept nothing less than the best performance from everyone.

Do leaders need to do other things throughout their day? Sure. They need to do many, many other things. Coaching is the one thing that takes priority over all other tactical needs. Winning leaders make time for it. They make it important. They do it continually throughout their days. They look for opportunities to do it. They seek it out. They balance it and prioritize it in their daily schedule.

So today, look at how you balance your time. Are your primary behaviors focused on tactical things? If the answer is yes, ask yourself, "If given the right amount of training and coaching, how much of these tactical things could be delegated to my team?" And then ask yourself, "If I did that, what "one thing" would I spend my extra time on?"

Was "more coaching" your answer? Congratulations if it was!

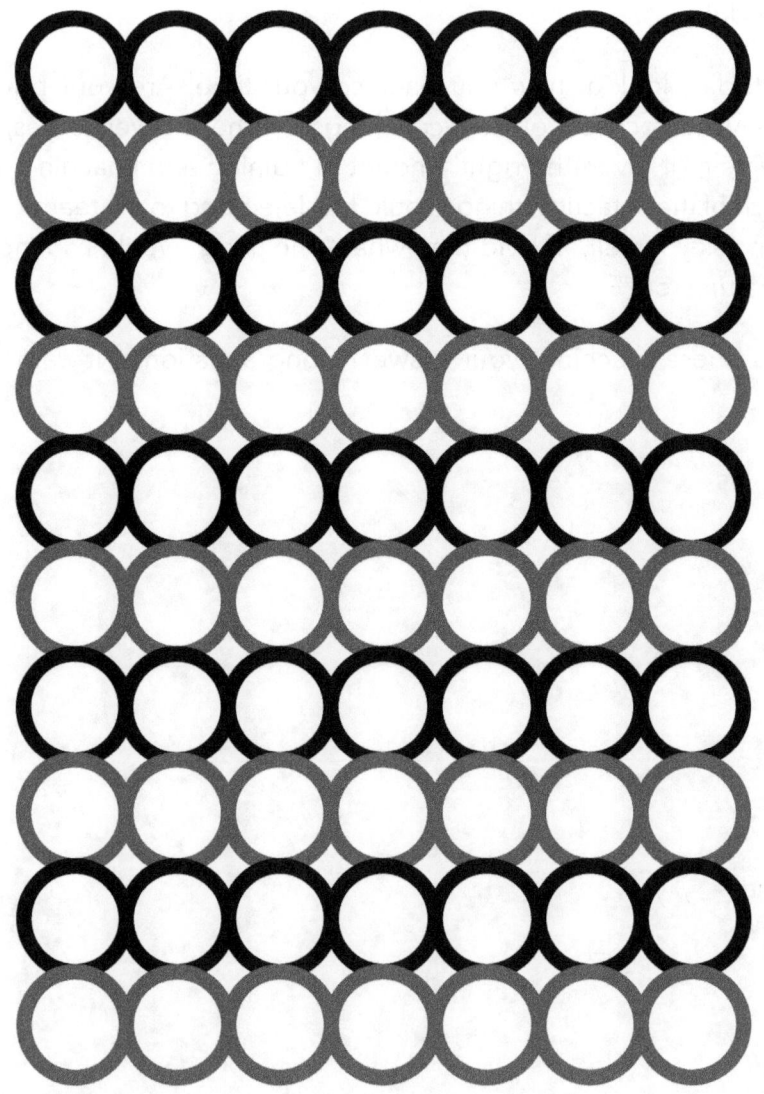

46 | THE POWER OF MOMENTUM

I have many favorite words. Kaizen (continuous improvement) was previously mentioned. Also, toward the top of this list is "Momentum." Why? Well, first, it's fun to say. Repeat it three times! See, I told you! Even the word itself gets me going. (If you start off slowly and then say it faster and faster it, you'll actually sound like a train.) A definition of the word "Momentum" *(driving power or strength)* reminds me of a train, too.

Momentum gives a train its movement. Think of how a train starts out from the station. Slowly, chug after chug after chug, it begins inching along. Straining to budge at first, but then it moves faster and faster and faster. Moving all that weight takes a concerted effort. It takes a lot of determination, it takes a lot of energy, it takes a lot of know-how, and it takes a lot of power.

But once that train starts moving, it gets easier and easier. It still takes power to keep it moving, but its momentum makes the train move faster and faster, and the power it ends up delivering as it moves is far greater than the power it consumes.

Getting the train powering forward takes a lot of time and effort, but...derailing it can happen in the blink of an eye.

Think about your lives and your teams in these terms. Think about all of the efforts you put in place to get your teams moving in the direction you want them to. You set them on the right track by providing them with training, coaching sessions and setting clear expectations. You keep them moving by giving them support and direction. You speed them up by lavishly praising their achievements and providing ongoing development.

Embrace the momentum. Embrace the movement. This leads to winning and success; however, the risk with any train is a derailment. This derailment could be caused by something large, but more likely, the derailment could be caused by something small. A winning conductor (leader) prepares for these dangers by seeking out training, leveraging the expertise of supervisors and peers, and watching out for the potential warning signs of danger ahead.

Another danger is the momentum moving the train backward or in the wrong direction. A winning conductor will then order the train to stop, reassess the destination and plans, and will then redirect it onto the right tracks.

Try as we might, sometimes, we find that we are heading backward or in the wrong direction, too. We then need to force ourselves and our teams to stop, reassess our objectives and expectations along with our business plans, and redirect everyone toward the desired destination.

Think about the team member who consistently outperforms the others. How are we encouraging their momentum to keep them moving? Are we giving them fuel (recognition)? Are we allowing them to mentor others?

Now, think about the team member who is moving in the wrong direction. How do we stop that negative momentum? Have we acknowledged it with them? Have we provided the expected behaviors (travel plans)? Have we given them the push (coaching/counseling) needed to move them in the right direction?

A train is only as powerful as its conductor. Its MOMENTUM is not provided by the coal. It's provided by the conductor who shovels it into the furnace.

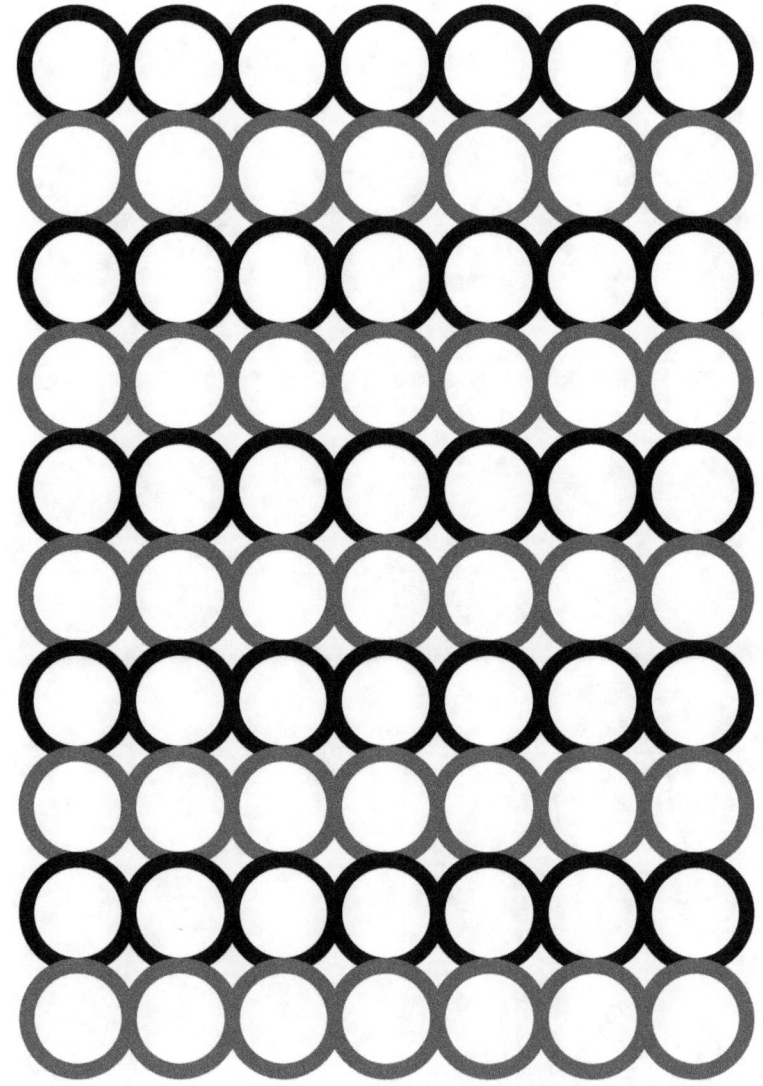

47 | THE TITANIC

I must admit it; the movie *"Titanic"* by James Cameron is still one of my favorites. I know that I may lose some "man points" by admitting it, but it's true. I love the scope of the movie, the storyline, and the wonderful visual production.

One of the underlying messages that is delivered by the history of the Titanic is that it doesn't matter how great the tactics are; it is the behaviors of the humans involved that deliver the results.

Just think about all the tactics that were in place with the Titanic. The design was state-of-the-art for its time. The hull was 882 feet long and was designed by some of the best minds in the industry. Its three propellers were driven by 29 steam engines that drove it at a speed of 23 knots (competitive even at today's standards). Its opulence is legendary. It had swimming pools, squash courts, libraries, and even a Turkish Spa. It was second to none in tactical design and structure.

But the over-confidence built by the tactics allowed for an unsafe level of performance on the high seas. As you all know, the ship struck an iceberg that ripped into the side of the hull and ultimately led to its sinking.

But the reason that it struck the iceberg wasn't the lack of execution on the designers' or builders' part; it was due to a simple lack of communication between the wireless operators and the ship's bridge. Two separate warnings of icebergs were communicated to the Titanic from other ships in the area, but the operators felt that they were "non-essential messages" and made the *conscious decision* not to pass the information along to the captain. Once the iceberg was spotted from the deck, it was too late.

In the world of leadership, many times, we also get so focused on developing new tactical approaches to drive the businesses that we overlook the level of execution from our team. We think that a new contest will get our team members to perform, or a new marketing strategy will create excitement in our customers. While both examples do impact our business and are crucial elements to strong organizations, the final results are ultimately up to our people. We can have the best-laid plans, but if they are not executed, the plans will fail. This fact is proven time after time, and the only way around it is through the behaviors of a winning leader.

The leader must ensure that their team knows what to do and how to do it. They need to ensure that they understand why and when things need to be done and are committed to the reasons behind what they do. And then they must ultimately take action on all the wonderful tactics that are put in place.

Moving the team to action is the ultimate behavior of a winning leader. While it's important that team members enjoy what they do, a contest or great strategy alone cannot replace an enjoyable culture that a winning leader creates every day.

In our world, we need to look at things holistically. Proper tactics need to be in place. We need to determine the appropriate steps that our team members need to take. We need to determine the appropriate marketing, financial, educational, operational, and technological processes. All these things are crucial to the stability and strength of an organization. But...then we need to determine the behavioral components and what we expect from the team members. Once they have the knowledge and skills and know the importance of their roles and the steps we want them to take, we need to ask ourselves, "Are their behaviors delivering the results that we want?" If not, we need to identify the correct performance gap and look at accountability.

The temptation is to keep re-examining the tactics. It is *emotionally* easier to create a new contest to drive results than it is to have a tough conversation with a team member who is choosing not to deliver to our level of expectations.

But perhaps the original tactics would work if the team members would perform.

The Titanic was built with world-class construction. No expense was spared. Still, on its very first voyage, it sank. Why? Because of the lack of proper execution.

Winning leaders set their teams up for winning results. They give them world-class tactics but also lead them to world-class performance!

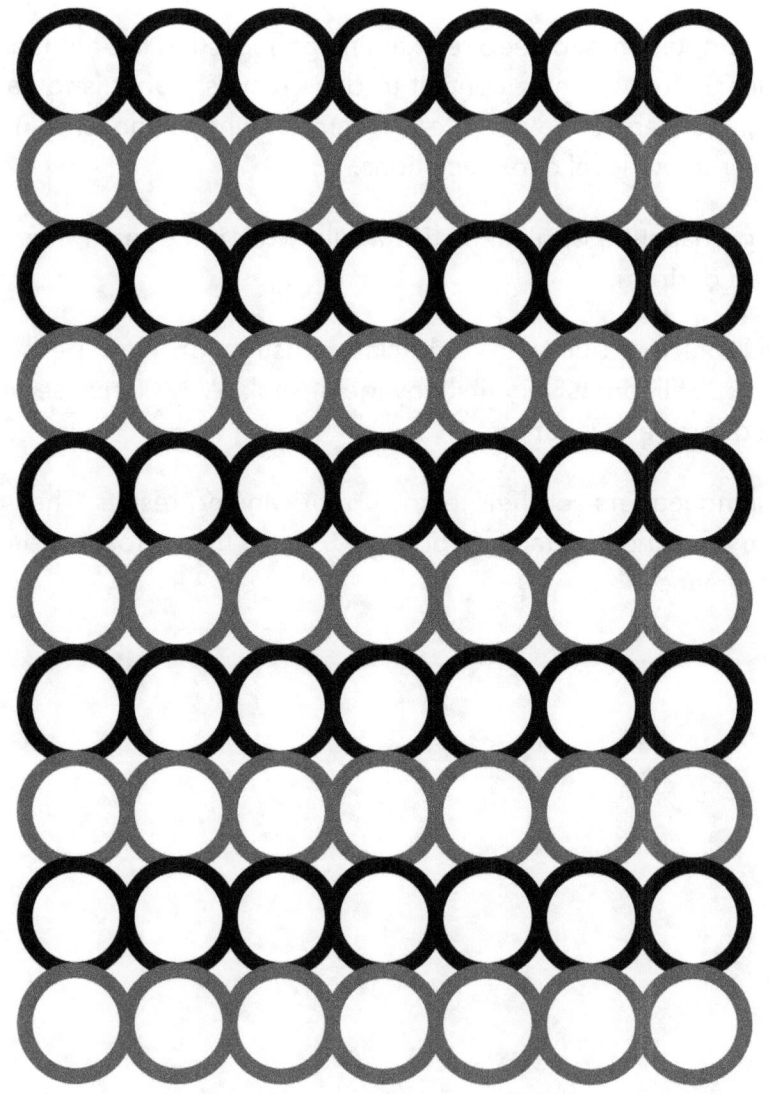

48 | TODAY

Nothing determines tomorrow more than today.

Why do many of us struggle with starting diet and exercise plans? We sit on the sofa in front of the television, watch the actors and actresses show off their six-pack abs, and think, "Man, I wish I was ripped like them!" We may even say, "Tomorrow, I'm going to start my diet," or "Tomorrow, I'm going to join the gym."

The problem stems not from the lack of commitment or ambition (although they are contributing factors) but from the "Tomorrow" mentality. We think it is ok to start things tomorrow or when it is more convenient.

To truly make the commitment to developing a healthy lifestyle, we must begin "Today." We cannot wait. We must start now. Call the gym and sign up. Go to the fridge or pantry and discard the junk and processed foods. Dump out the alcohol and throw out the cigarettes. Call a friend to join in your commitment. Take action today to build momentum for tomorrow.

The same thought process is used by winning leaders every day. They look at their objectives and result expectations through the lens of "Today."

"What specific behaviors will determine success in my role today? What Gaps exist today? Who needs training today? Who needs development today? What are the talent levels needed today? Whom do I need to communicate with, and what methods are needed today? Whom can I motivate today? Who doesn't understand the priorities today? How can I clarify and reinforce expectations today? Where do I need to create accountability today? What is the culture, and how can I influence it today? Today, who is committed to winning and who isn't?"

Winning leaders ask questions like these to themselves every day. They are concerned with long-term result expectations that deliver key objectives, but where they differ from many other leaders is how they go after the answers. They begin with today. They don't get caught up in successes or failures from yesterday; they don't put things off or worry about tomorrow. They understand that each day is an opportunity to determine their future, and each day must be strategically leveraged to achieve their desired outcomes.

After the questions are asked and the answers are discovered, action is taken. Winning leaders don't just ask them and wait until next week to meet about the answers. They take action today. They discover the answers, who's accountable, who can influence change, and who can be rewarded. They start training and teaching now to develop the talent. They communicate their expectations today, validate that their message is received, and then investigate that the behaviors are being acted upon immediately and correctly. They establish priorities and ensure that every member of the organization understands them, believes in them, and acts upon them right from the start. They make necessary and immediate changes to any of their own behaviors that detract from their desired cultural environment where a teaching organization is built upon trust and commitment.

In this fast-paced world, we live in, there is no time to waste. Each moment, each day, must be acted upon. We cannot wait until tomorrow to take action. When key, monumental decisions need to be made, we must stop and make sure that the action is the right action, but once we've determined what that right action is, we must take it.

There is no better time than the present for action.

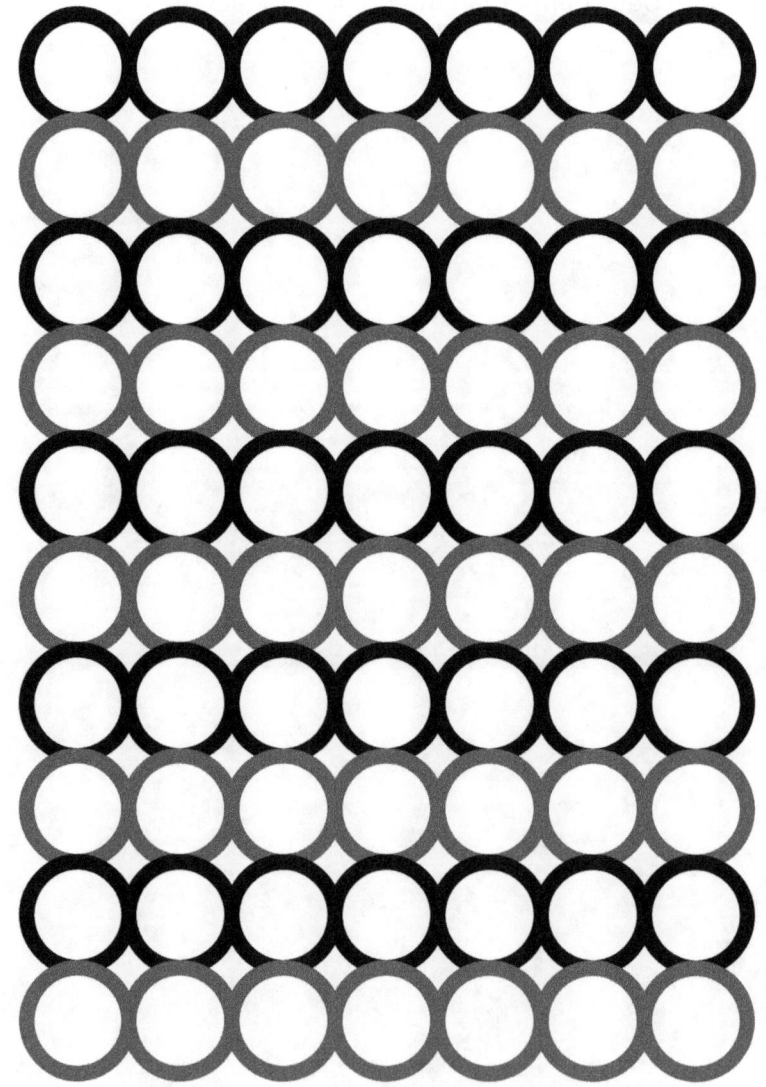

49 | TOUGH LOVE

What would you do? As a parent, your son or daughter gets involved with the wrong crowd and starts doing drugs. Your best friend misses work regularly due to a drinking problem. Your spouse shows signs of an eating disorder.

Many people just ignore the situation and hope that the behaviors go away. They close their eyes and hearts to the destructiveness and pretend nothing is wrong. The love they feel for the individual is too strong for them to challenge them in any way that might cause an argument or split the relationship into two.

Others practice a form of "Tough Love" with them. They sternly confront their loved ones and force them to change their behaviors using abrasive and radical methods. These people leverage Tough Love's "tough" part more than the "love" part.

Some people, however, understand that Tough Love needs to be built from equal parts of toughness and love. It must be a true blend of the two parts. Without strong words and actions, the person struggling will often not see the path that he or she is on. They will continue heading blindly down the road to destruction and ruin. Conversely, without empathy, compassion, love, and support, the relationship may tend to crumble under pressure, leaving both parties alone and on their own to handle the situation.

True tough love comes from a place of support where the victims of addiction or negative behaviors feel challenged yet supported by the ones he or she cares for.

Winning leaders behave in much the same way when building a culture of action in a learning organization. They offer their team members two options. One option is performing to the leader's expectations and achieving the objectives. The other option is to be successful somewhere else. They provide these two options in a culture of support.

Winning leaders train, teach and hire the best talent in the world. They set high behavioral and result expectations and clearly communicate the priorities around the things that truly matter. They create accountability and build commitment in a culture of action. They are very clear that only winning results will be accepted.

They also do all these things while providing immensely strong support for the team he or she builds. Winning leaders are determined that their teams will succeed, and they understand that the team member will struggle without support from the leader. "Struggle" is not a word that a winning leader embraces on their team. They avoid it at all costs. They talk to their team, asking specifically for areas where the team needs support. They look for these areas by monitoring results and behaviors in the real world. They reach out and offer suggestions that may lead a team member in the right direction; when required, they handle the situation in a tough manner. They don't back down from struggles or challenges; they attack them. They solve them. They make the situations better. They turn complaints into compliments.

Winning leaders don't accept that their team members struggle. They look at their own behavior first to see if they have created a performance gap. Do they know what to do and how to do it? Do they know why and when something needs to be done? Have they transferred ownership of taking action and created a culture of commitment and accountability?

If the answer is "no" to these questions, the leader steps back and closes the Performance Gaps firmly and completely.

If the answer is "yes," the winning leader uses his or her EDGE (Energy, Decisiveness, Greatness, and Expectations) to move the team member to a position off their team. They set high standards and communicate expectations and feedback so effectively that the team member knows they must choose to be successful somewhere else if they can't meet those standards. No hard feelings...no drama...just the realization that this team accepts only the best and those who strive to be just that.

They know that their winning leader is leading. Leading with Tough Love.

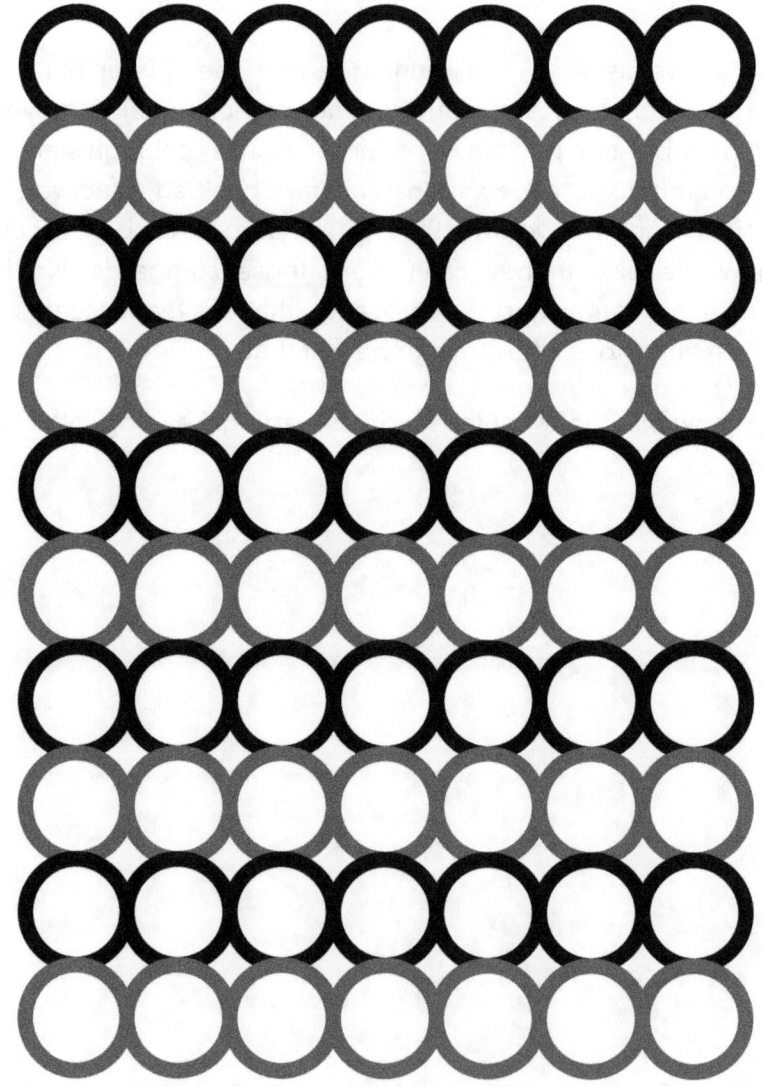

50 | WANTS AND NEEDS

My boys gave me a great thought last Christmas when we discussed their lists for Santa. What is the difference between "Wants and Needs"? Children get these two things mixed up a lot…

- "I NEED a new Xbox!"

- "I NEED a new guitar!"

- "I NEED a new car!"

Their requests made me think… "Santa NEEDS more money!"

It also made me think about the difference between "wants and needs." Do my boys truly "need" those things? Are they a matter of life and death? Would the world stop without them? Obviously, the answer is no (My answer to them was "no," too!). To their dismay, I entered my Trainer role and had them define the different elements of "wants and needs." (They just love this side of me!)

In our world, do our team members understand the differences? When we tell them, "I need you to do this…" do they understand that their jobs and our business success depend on it? Now, of course, you don't have to explain it in those particular terms, but they need to come to grips with the level of importance of each behavioral expectation.

Actually, we need to come to grips with this as well. It is up to us as leaders to communicate the importance levels of our expectations. Do the team members understand if the action is important to our results? Do they know that the request isn't a "want" but a "need"?

Their confusion or lack of performance often results from our communication being unclear. We need to reflect on the items on our weekly and daily priority lists and decide which ones are "wants" and which are "needs" and then use that decision to communicate our direction appropriately and clearly.

So often, we have a million items on our plates, and we just keep feeding those things to our teams. One after the other, we just direct and direct and direct without providing any level of importance to each item. We then leave the decision of creating the priority list to our team members. Then, when they don't complete the item that we feel is the most important, we blame them. We create the Importance Gap!

It's not their fault that they didn't know the difference between OUR "wants and needs." We never communicated that to them.

We need to slow down, reflect on our own "wants and needs," determine which actions are most important and which can wait, and then clearly and completely communicate that priority list to our team members.

This way, our "NEEDS" get met, and then we can work on our "WANTS" …like a new iPhone for Santa! (I wonder where my kids get it.)

51 | WINNERS HIRE WINNERS

It's amazing. We've witnessed it time and time again. Underperformers hire underperformers. Mediocre performers hire mediocre performers. Winners hire winners.

The often-quoted Jim Collins got it right in his book, *"Good to Great,"* when he said, "Get the right people on the bus."[5] If we want great results, we need to get great people on our bus. This process, of course, starts with the leader.

Winning leaders recognize greatness in people and know how to leverage great people for the betterment of the overall team. They understand what makes a person tick, what motivates them, and what drives them to consistently exceed expectations. Most importantly, however, is that winning leaders know how to surround themselves with talented winners.

If we, as leaders, live in a world of mediocrity, we will struggle with seeing a winning vision. We won't know what "great" is and, therefore, we will continue to be satisfied to hire the "warm body" that will just fill the immediate hole in our roster without any regard

---

[5] Collins, Jim. Good to Great. Harper Business, 2001.

for talent and trainability. We will just be happy to have the shift covered so we can continue to stay afloat.

Mediocre leaders take a mediocre approach to hiring by looking primarily for things like basic skills, availability, and if they seem to be a "nice" person. They don't dig deeply into truly what this person can contribute to the organization, how they will fit into the team and how they will push the group's overall results to an even higher level.

"Will this person improve the overall team, lower it, or keep it at the same level?" Winning leaders ask this question of themselves when they are interviewing a candidate for their team.

As their overall mission is to consistently improve the team members' behaviors, move them to action and ultimately improve their results, the winning leader identifies specific behavioral indicators in each candidate they interview. They make a firm decision that if the person isn't going to improve their team's results, they won't hire them.

We've found that winning leaders do this best by ranking their teams. They determine who their "A" players, "B" players, and "C" players are. They determine who their stars are and at what level they have acceptable performance. They identify the specific person on their current roster who is their lowest-performing associate and who is still performing at an acceptable level. This is where they set their

ABC RANKING	TEAM POSITION	TEAM MEMBER NAME	ACCEPTABILITY BAR LEVEL
A-PLAYERS	1		
	2		STAR PLAYER BAR LEVEL
	3		
B-PLAYERS	4		
	5		ACCEPTABLE PLAYER BAR LEVEL
	6		
C-PLAYERS	7		
	8		UNACCEPTABLE PLAYER BAR LEVEL
	9		
	10		

"acceptability bar." This level is where they've determined all new hires *must* immediately perform at once given the appropriate training. No one will ever be hired at a level below his or her lowest acceptable player.

The beauty of this method is that the team's overall performance continues to improve. As higher-level players are introduced to the team, the acceptability bar continues to move up. Also, by intentionally using this strategic method, leaders are less likely to hire someone just because they are desperate or hire someone because they are "nice."

If we have a team of mediocre performers, we must identify which Gap contributes to this result. If we identify that a Knowledge Gap is the cause, we must review our hiring practices and the overall talent level of our team. Where are we setting our bars? What interviewing steps are we following? Are there specific competencies we look for? Are the interviewing tools we use designed around the competencies? Do we use other less tangible things like Core Values as a measuring stick? Do we ask behavioral questions seeking evidence of past performance, transferable skills, and overall results? Then do we determine our acceptability bar level for our current team and commit to only hiring someone who will perform at a higher level?

Winning leaders understand these things and believe completely in them. They know that hiring a winning team member depends entirely upon their own winning performance in the hiring process. The bar is set high, the commitment to the process is set high, and their results, ultimately, are high.

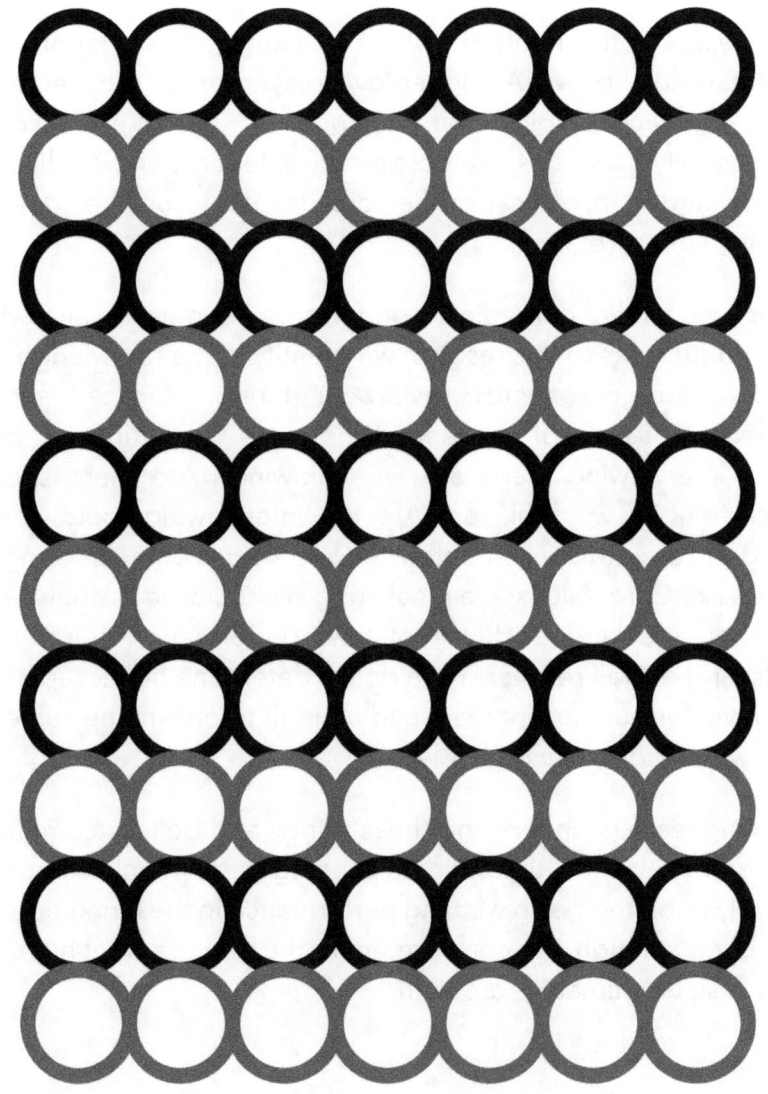

52 | WORK SMARTER, NOT HARDER

I'm sure you've heard this phrase, *"Work Smarter, Not Harder"*. It might seem like common sense too. However, when it comes to our daily work lives, many of us muscle our way through them. We tend to use the skills from our past role that made us successful in our current role, and we may not even realize that the required skill set changed.

We just work harder and harder. We work more and more hours. We see our family and friends less and less. And as a result, we actually get less and less done. We then burn ourselves out (and many times take our teams with us!).

We don't realize that we need to slow down to speed up.

Stephen R. Covey describes this phenomenon as one of the key habits in his best-selling book *"The Seven Habits of Highly Effective People."*[6] Here is the story as he described:

> *A man was struggling in the woods to saw down a tree. An old farmer came by, watched for a while, then quietly said, "What are you doing?"*

---

[6] Covey, Stephen R. <u>Seven Habits of Highly Effective People</u>. Revised Edition (November 9, 2004). Free Press, 2004.

"Can't you see?" the man impatiently replied, "I'm sawing down this tree."

"You look exhausted," said the farmer. "How long have you been at it?"

"Over five hours, and I'm beat," replied the man. "This is hard work."

"That saw looks pretty dull," said the farmer. "Why don't you take a break for a few minutes and sharpen it? I'm sure it would go a lot faster."

"I don't have time to sharpen the saw," the man says emphatically.

"I'm too busy sawing!"

As leaders, to sharpen our own saws, we need to:

- Take some time (one hour daily) to analyze and prioritize what our weekly/daily result expectations are...Weekly first...then daily...

- Determine what specific behavioral expectations are necessary to achieve those expectations.

- Evaluate previous/current performance...good and bad.

  o Bad: What behaviors produced that result? What behaviors should have been in place to get us the result we desire? What prevented the behaviors from happening?

  o Good: What behavior produced that result? Why were those behaviors executed?

- Determine what specific steps are necessary to reverse bad results and repeat good results.

- Develop the plan and put it into place (adjusting weekly/daily based on results).

As winning leaders, we are expected to lead. Lead people, lead processes, lead strategies which all lead to results. We are no longer only task performers. Yes, part of being a leader is leading by example, but that is only a part. We are also expected to strategically lead our teams down a path of continued improvement and continued success. We need to do this by closing Knowledge Gaps, Importance Gaps and Action Gaps.

This means we need sharpen our saws to work *smart* before we can work *hard*.

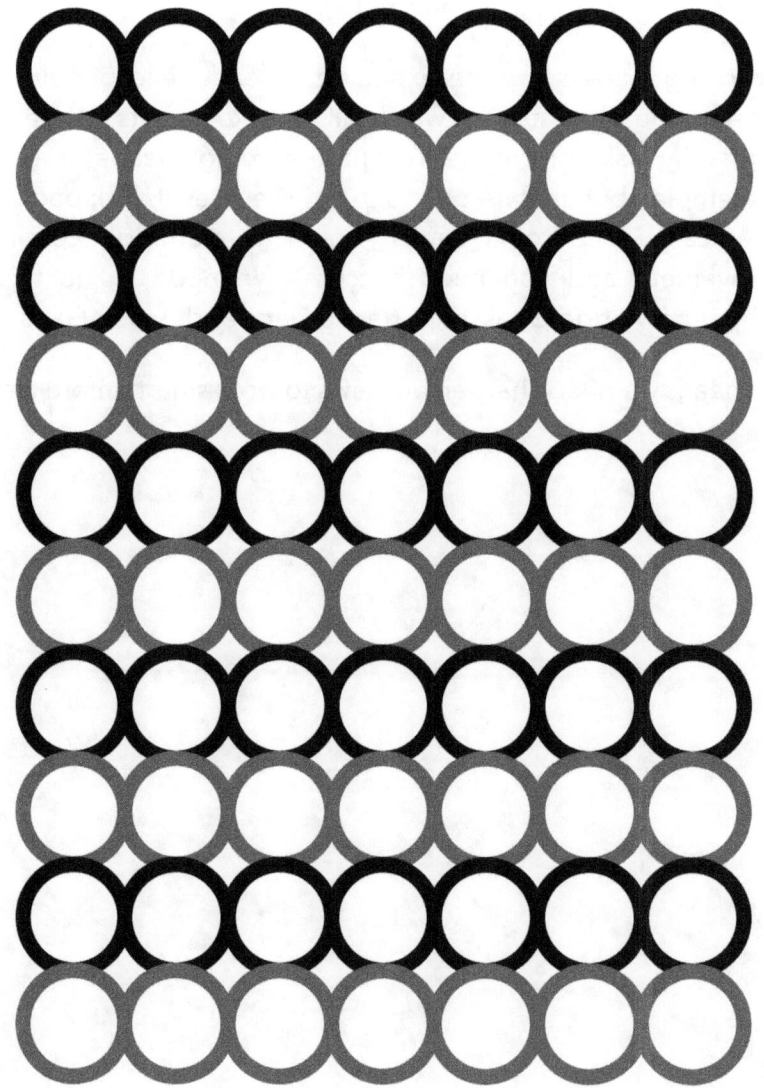

FINAL WORDS

One common theme laid out throughout this book is the power of choosing to take action. There can be no winning without it; there can be no winning leaders without it. Winning requires someone making the choice to take action around the specific, verified steps that <u>will</u> lead to the result that they expect. All championship performances have been built from this premise.

Coaches, business leaders, and political leaders all understand that for their organizations to be successful, they must determine the specific steps that will deliver the outcomes they want, and then they must put those steps into play. Doing so requires the team members to know what to do and how to do it, they must understand why the steps are important and when those steps must be taken, and finally, the team members must choose to take the action. Taking action on specific steps is paramount to the success of the process, and a strong, willing leader must lead the team through it.

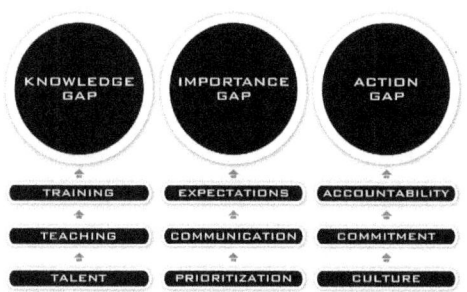

Along the way, the leader and his or her team will experience Performance Gaps. Team members will not know what to do or how to do things, they will not know why or when those things need to be done, and there will be individuals who make the conscious or unconscious choice not to take the action. There will be Knowledge Gaps, Importance Gaps, and Action Gaps. This is a fact of life…a fact of working in the human world.

What winning leaders do, however, is quickly identify these Gaps and effectively close them. In doing so, they minimize the risks created by the Gaps and maximize their teams' potential. Everything, however, begins with the leader being willing and able to do so.

Understanding, believing, and being committed to the Gapology method will create the ability to lead through the Gaps…taking action will deliver the results. Choose to take action… and enjoy your journey as a winning leader!

WORKS CITED

Bridges, William. <u>Managing Transitions</u>. Third Edition. Da Capo Lifelong Books, 2009.

Collins, Jim. <u>Good To Great</u>. Harper Business, 2001.

Consumer Reports.Org. <u>Consumer Reports</u>. January 2008. 17 July 2011 <Http://Www.Consumerreports.Org/Cro/Cars/New-Cars/News/2008/01/Brand-Perceptions/Overview/Brand-Perceptions-Top-5.Htm>.

Covey, Stephen R. <u>Seven Habits Of Highly Effective People</u>. Revised Edition (November 9, 2004). Free Press, 2004.

Mark Thienes, Brian Brockhoff. <u>Gapology: How Winning Leaders Close Performance Gaps</u>. Universal Publishers, 2010.

Maxwell, John C. <u>The Right To Lead</u>. Thomas Nelson, 2010.

Ph.D., Richard Carlson. <u>Don't Sweat The Small Stuff...And It's All Small Stuff</u>. Hyperion, 1996.

Robbins, Anthony. <u>Awaken The Giant Within</u>. Free Press, 1992.

Tulgan, Bruce. <u>It's Okay To Be The Boss</u>. Harper Business, 2007.

Tv Guide. "Tv Guide's 50 Greatest Tv Shows Of All Time." <u>Tv Guide</u> 4-10 May 2002.

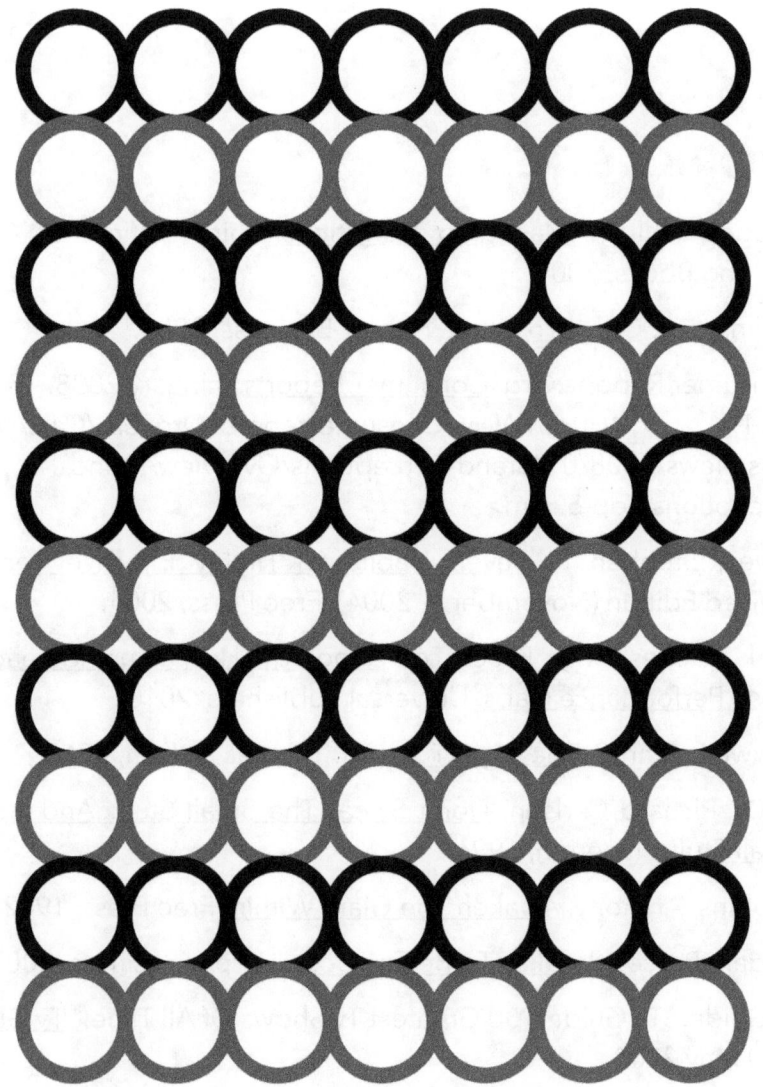

ACKNOWLEDGMENTS

Friends come and go. Mentors come and go. Many people don't always realize that in their "coming and going," lives change. My life has changed because of each one of them. I am the man who I am because of them. I am a leader, writer, mentor, coach, and inspiration because of them. For this reason, I extend my deepest and most heartfelt gratitude and love.

Thank you goes to Mark Thienes, without whom none of my writing dreams would have been accomplished…or even attempted.

Thank you also to my beautiful wife Jolyann whose passion for life and clarity around the world's Gaps (including ones that I own) gives me reason to strive to be my ultimate best. She is an example of who I want to be.

Thank you to my boys…or, more correctly, young men…Jesse, Jonas, and Jacob, you inspire me to work hard and love even harder.

Thank you to my parents, sister, brother, in-laws, extended family, and friends as they continue demonstrating unending support.

To other champions of Gapology, I thank you for giving Gapology its first voice in the world.

To all our new readers, we thank you for putting Gapology in your life and making it a powerful tool in your winning leadership.

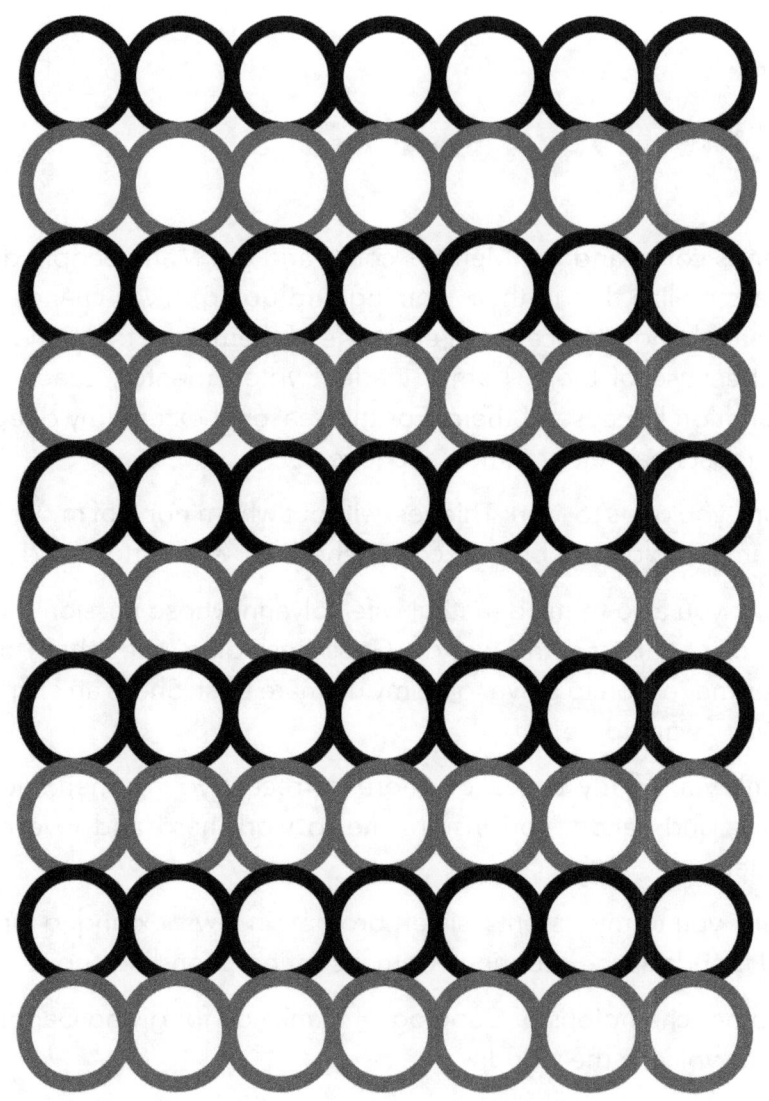

ENDORSEMENTS

"Gapology is more than a business book that I have read; it has become the reference guide that I turn to daily. Incorporating the concepts & practices into my leadership rhythm has enabled me to deliver sustained "Best" results. I have had the privilege of having Brian be my Coach and Mentor throughout the past few years and his insight…and questions…. have led me to breakthrough performance.

Now, Brian has packaged his learnings throughout his leadership and training journey into "Gapology Inspirations". These are great stories that everyone can relate to; and they reinforce the positive power of leadership. What a perfect way to start out each new Monday morning with a Winning Spirit!!

Brian is truly driven by the desire to help leaders and their teams reach their full potential…. I promise you that putting Gapology into action will certainly help you achieve yours!"

-Brenda Beasley, DSM Chico's FAS

"Gapology Inspirations" is a book that really taps into the two major radio stations that every book should tap into: "WII-FM" and "MMFI-AM". *"WII-FM" = "What's In It For Me" and "MMFI-AM" = "Make Me Feel Important About Myself"*. I think everyone should read the book, as there is something for everyone and their own radio stations! A great read for sure in these tough times."

-Doug McCallum, President, McCallum and Associates, Inc. International Training and Consulting Company, Lincoln, Nebraska

Gapology Inspirations is a great companion to Thienes and Brockhoff's first book, *Gapology: How Winning Leaders Close Performance Gaps*. This book is packed with stories and examples that are both interesting and thought provoking. What a great way to help leaders see the practical application and improve leadership capability.

-Wayne Vandewater, VP – Learning and Development, Applebee's

ABOUT THE AUTHOR

Brian Brockhoff, Co-Founder, President & Creative Director of Gapology Institute, has led and mentored teams of diverse business leaders for over thirty years and is responsible for the creation and design of numerous skill-development programs.

Brian designed and co-authored *Gapology: How Winning Leaders Close Performance Gaps*, *IMBAR: The Pathway of Transformation*, and *Speed of Purpose: Achieve 2.8X Productivity and Beyond* with

Mark Thienes. They both host the podcast series, *Gapology Radio*. Brian writes *The Gapology Angle* blog series, on which these books are based, and he has also produced online training courses on topics from this book.

Gapology Products and Services

Visit www.gapology.org for full details on
Gapology Institute Workshops and Coaching Services

Books

Gapology: How Winning Leaders Close Performance Gaps

IMBAR: The Pathway of Transformation

Speed of Purpose: Achieve 2.8X Productivity and Beyond

Gapology Inspirations

Gapology Workbook

Also

Audible e-book: Gapology: How Winning Leaders Close
Performance Gaps

Online Training Course on Udemy.com: Gapology: How Winning
Leaders Close Performance Gaps

Podcast: Gapology Radio

Blog: The Gapology Angle

Social too!

Connect with us on LinkedIn, Facebook, Instagram, or Pinterest.

www.ingramcontent.com/pod-product-compliance
Lightning Source LLC
Chambersburg PA
CBHW071715170526
45165CB00005B/2019